D0382364

into the **Primitive environment**

into the
Primitive environment

by Robert Brain

Prentice-Hall Inc. Englewood Cliffs New Jersey

Original U.S. Edition published by
Prentice-Hall, Inc., Englewood Cliffs, New Jersey

Copyright © Text Robert Brain 1972

All rights reserved

Made by Roxby Press Productions
55 Conduit Street London W1R 9FD England
Editor Michael Leitch
Picture research Ann Usborne
Design and art direction Ivan and Robin Dodd

Printed in Great Britain by Oxley Press Limited

ISBN: 0-13-477174-5

Library of Congress Catalog Card No: 72-4328

Contents

THE ROAD TO EXTINCTION

This book is about simple societies. Its theme is the various ways in which cultures seen to be different from our own have been and are being destroyed. Most of the groups which we commonly call 'primitive' will have disappeared within one generation from now unless drastic measures are taken to arrest this tragic process. Their collapse has come about chiefly through the pitiless demands made by western industrialized society on land, resources and people. A major purpose of this book is to ask whether it is in fact feasible to help isolated, exotic cultures to survive in the modern world, even to the extent of protecting them in their 'uncivilized' modes of life; or whether all the minority peoples of this planet must now radically change their way of life, or die.

First Contacts

Contact between Europe and the rest of the world, between isolated tribes, island communities and 'lost' civilizations, began with the waning of the Middle Ages, when five small European countries (Portugal, Spain, Holland, Britain and France) became extraordinarily aggressive and sent forth explorers, traders, empire-builders and missionaries into the 'uncivilized' world. At the turn of the nineteenth century, along with the great industrial and social revolutions, contact became intensive between Europe and the rest of the world, between civilized and primitive forms of existence. If the latter did not immediately adapt or at least provide healthy markets for the white men's goods, they were harassed and persecuted, forcibly converted to the white man's ways or wilfully exterminated. Countless cultures, faced with the steamrolling impact of an intolerant Europe, quickly disappeared – either because their members were exterminated or because their culture was assimilated. Of most of these people nothing remains but a few dusty relics in museums; others have managed to survive either in isolation or in contact with larger societies. Many more are today in imminent danger of extermination, their future conditioned by factors that were in operation a century ago.

In any study of societies which have undergone or are undergoing the traumatic experience of contact with European culture, it is astonishing how constant has been the pattern of conquest and the reaction to it. First came

exploration and settlement; these stages were followed by exploitation, expropriation of native land, decimation of the population and its forced conversion to the ways of living and religion of the conquerors. They in turn led to the eventual disappearance of both the race and the culture. Fortunately not all societies travelled the whole of this disastrous road; some, through their own initiative or through consideration and guidance on the part of their invaders, have been able to adapt to the modern situation. Most, however, did not.

At this stage we should also remember that the Europeans are not the only villains. Since the world began technologically superior peoples have exploited and enslaved people less fortunate than themselves: to the Greeks, the Romans, the Egyptians and Mesopotamians it was an automatic process that accompanied conquest. In more recent times other masters have inflicted subjection on the Middle East, on the Ainus in Japan, the Negritos in the Philippines and the Dayaks in Indonesia. In some societies, too, it has been customary to maintain sub-groups on whom

the ills of society at large are projected; members of the sub-group are in effect scapegoats and are treated as objects of contempt: Gipsies, Hindu Untouchables, Hawaiian outcastes – they and many others have been accused of somehow contaminating the lives of the majority group.

Throughout history peoples of different cultures have considered themselves to be as different from each other as dog from cat. To the Greeks and Romans 'savages' and 'barbarians' were epithets for people living outside their own boundaries; and it is common for people of one culture to think of those along the road, over the river or behind the mountain as 'not quite human', and therefore legitimate targets for head-hunting, abduction and slave raids. Until our present century this kind of xenophobia, or fear of strangers, was well-nigh universal. In Africa the names of many tribes meant simply 'we, the people', 'the men': everyone else was different; and fantastic notions circulated about neighbouring peoples who 'walked on their heads', ate their children, could not walk because of their

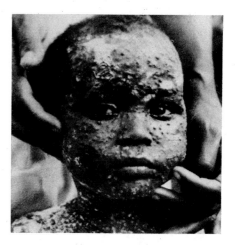

previous page By 1967 the Txikao, a Brazilian tribe, were reduced from over 400 (1960) to a mere fifty-three. These boys are some of the survivors who were taken into the Xingu National Park, a scheme which at present protects some 1,500 Indians. **opposite, above** Colonial stereotypes – two empire-builders and a 'savage' – from Cape Colony, c. 1880. **opposite, below** Ainu entertainers, remnants of an ancient subject people, receive Japanese visitors to their village, Shiraoi, on Hokkaido. **this page** Colonial expansion brought numerous fatal diseases that decimated native populations – even colds and measles were deadly among isolated peoples who lacked our immunity to them. Here, Eskimos wear masks for protection against tuberculosis; the African boy is a smallpox victim.

above Alcohol was one white export that received a big welcome wherever it was made available; this photograph was taken in a village near Kumasi, Ghana. **right** Mealtime on an Indian Protection Service reserve, Brazil. Deficiencies in diet caused problems in many areas; the European food that was distributed was often of poor quality, and natives were deprived of necessary vitamins.

heavy heads, or whose sons often married their mothers.

The Europeans, too, developed just these attitudes towards the peoples they came upon and conquered. This was particularly true of the English during their proud days when Queen Victoria ruled the waves and half the map of the world was painted red. To them the stereotype by which they identified particular groups of natives varied according to the relationship between the natives and themselves. To the explorers he was a 'noble savage', to the settler a 'murdering wretch', to the soldier a 'filthy coward', to the missionary a 'poor misguided child', to the planter a 'lazy, good-for-nothing nigger'. All the stereotypes had one element in common: they vividly expressed the white man's need to believe in his own superiority.

The creation of the myth that one sector of humanity was 'civilized' while another was 'primitive', together with the invention of stereotypes to characterize the inferiority of invaded peoples, was in many cases the prelude to acts of abominable cruelty. The aggression of the invader frequently amounted to a policy of outright extermination; sadistic acts abounded as the vanquished were tormented and then all too often dispatched in large numbers.

After the first and usually violent stage of contact, however, there often followed a still more disastrous period when the people were decimated by new diseases introduced among them by the invader; a psychological decline then set in, accompanied by a loss of the will to live. At this point the conquering race assumed that the primitives were doomed to die and used this assumption as an excuse for neglecting them.

Disease and Despair

Illnesses introduced by Europeans took a terrible toll of the peoples inhabiting the lands that were discovered, exploited and settled in the eighteenth and nineteenth centuries. One of the few experts in this field, A. Grenfell Price, writes: 'Taken as a whole a great mass of evidence indicates that the diseases of the invaders and of their labour forces were a powerful factor, perhaps in some cases the most powerful factor, in the defeat of the indigenous peoples and not infrequently in their destruction.' Where the natives were few, and had no natural resistance to smallpox and tuberculosis, measles and leprosy, the destruction was horrific, at least until modern medicine was available to them or some kind of immunity could be established – enough, in some cases, to lead to recovery and population growth. The effects of what we think of as innocuous illnesses – the

right Macusi Indian children at a mission
in British Guiana (now Guyana). Despite the
many good works of the missionaries,
they also undoubtedly caused a great deal
of harm. They did this in many places by
suppressing the old religious and cultural
systems of the natives without properly
considering either their value or the
consequences of doing so; and by their
over-anxiety to secure converts to
Christianity when their help was more
urgently needed in such fields as health and
education. Among the customs banned by
missionaries were pig-feasting in New
Guinea, surfing in Hawaii, and dancing in
parts of Africa (below). below right A
chief of the Canelos Indians of Ecuador with
his top hat and silver cane, adopted as marks
of his authority.

common cold, influenza, whooping cough, measles and chicken pox – were often disastrous to isolated peoples who had never before come into contact with them, and for whom they become scourges of the worst kind.

In addition, the general vigour of subjected populations tended to decrease through deficiencies in diet; the European food that was distributed to the natives was often lacking in quality, balance and vitamins, and so rendered its consumers more susceptible to disease.

Psychological factors also intervened. Apathy, loss of zest or the will to live meant that resistance to illness was seriously diminished. The so-called social diseases, syphilis and gonorrhoea, were also introduced and became major enemies of fertility and hence a prime cause in the decline of peoples who experienced an almost continuous sexual invasion from sailors, soldiers, whalers, sealers and traders. These roving men found themselves separated from their own women for years on end, and almost habitually engaged in orgies of sexual licence with the women, willing or otherwise, of the conquered race.

Undoubtedly, in the first days of explorations and settlement such consequences could not have been foreseen and the white settlers could not be held morally responsible for the diseases they unwittingly transmitted. However there is irrefutable evidence that some settlers, hungry for land, found room to expand by deliberately killing off natives with diseases which were sometimes purposefully introduced. Smallpox virus, for example, could be – and was – wiped on gifts of cloth intended for unsuspecting natives. Germ warfare of this nature, appalling and sensational as it may appear, has been documented both in the past (Tasmania) and the present (South America); these cases are more fully discussed later in this chapter and in Chapter 2.

The Gifts of Civilization
Traders and whalers not only brought disease, they also filled the native with alcohol, usually as a means of payment for local goods. To peoples unused to fermented drinks, this was universally disastrous: gin, whisky and rum were

immediately appreciated and became a craving. They had no more immunity against the ravages of alcohol than they did against chickenpox; only a small intake was needed for immediate drunkenness. Violence often followed.

It was the missionaries who introduced another danger: clothing. In many primitive societies (and in our own, too, in some cases) clothes were and are worn for symbolic reasons, not because men were ashamed of their nakedness, nor to protect them against the cold. The Tasmanians, for example, despite the very cold climate in which they lived, went entirely naked. With the arrival of the missionaries clothes were immediately put on their pagan backs, to suit the moral and symbolic purposes of the Christians. To be converted a 'native' of any country had to wear clothes, decided the missionaries; but many did not stop to consider whether such clothes might not be a source of danger to a previously naked tribe, especially in hot climates where a loin cloth was sufficient. They also failed to teach the people that their clothes should occasionally be washed. Consequently they were never removed until they were in filthy tatters and a haven for vermin. Nor did 'natives' know that they should change their clothes when they became wet; so they slept in them and developed pneumonia, chest complaints and other illnesses.

It is fairly easy to evaluate the effects of murder, disease and alcohol. It is harder to assess the results of the devaluation and contempt which dominant groups showed towards the cultures of the primitive peoples they conquered and which inevitably resulted in their disintegration. For this the missionaries have been held largely to blame, in many cases with justice.

While we should appreciate the missionaries' good intentions, their self-sacrifices in the cause of 'saving souls for Jesus', and the many occasions when they protected their converts from the rapacity of settlers and governments, it is also true that they were remarkably short-sighted in their aims and showed a high degree of moral arrogance. They hardly ever studied the religious and cultural systems of the natives with what we would now call a proper sympathy. A people's religious heritage would be cast aside, but nothing so *deeply* moving was put in its place.

The missionaries attacked the prestige and status of elders and chiefs by banning certain types of marriage, and bridewealth, and by supporting children against their fathers. They banned pig-feasting in New Guinea, drinking and smoking in South America, dancing in Africa. In Hawaii they even prohibited surfing. The words 'chastity'

left Girl with plastic bowl, Liberia.
above, top Reserves – even when they are less degrading than this South African corral for unwanted Africans and political prisoners – create more problems than they can ever solve. **above** Nigerian cowboys. Somewhere the legends of the Wild West have taken a strange turning.

right Tasmanians recorded in the journal of Abel Janszoon Tasman, who discovered them in 1642. Until 1835 the island was known as Van Diemen's Land after Tasman's patron. **below right** Engraving of a Tasmanian boy, made towards the end of the eighteenth century.

and 'fornication' were forever on their pale lips. On the whole, few missionaries succeeded in appreciating the significance of traditional institutions; everything western and Christian was good, everything native and pagan was bad. These aspects of cultural disturbance are discussed more fully in Chapter 3, 'The Landeaters', which looks in particular at events in Australia and North America.

The Settlers Take Over

Missionaries are an easy target for attack, and while they undoubtedly made many blind mistakes, these counted for little compared to the consequences of economic exploitation and the harsh measures of foreign administrators. The greatest threat which native peoples faced from colonialism was the expropriation of their lands and the removal of their livelihood. Settlers from Europe found vast and fertile countries inhabited by a few weak and divided peoples; and if these peoples did not make way for the technologically superior invaders, they were replaced by hardier and more complacent workers from other countries. This situation was repeated in a remarkably similar pattern in Australia, New Zealand and North and South America (see Chapter 2).

Reserves

Colonial governments and the administrators of subject peoples often contrived to complete the havoc which disease, the missionary and the settler had begun. The most efficient method of removing 'dangerous' natives was to place them in prisons, in reserves or Bantustans – call them what you will. In almost every case mentioned in this book the conquered 'primitive' peoples were either forcibly pushed into unproductive corners of the environment by the rapacious modern farmer, or were placed in reserves put aside specially for them. These reserves invariably aimed at keeping the natives off the lands appropriated by the invaders. At least in theory the system would not necessarily have been unworkable if the land designated had been adequate, and if the arrangement had been intended to protect the natives' interests against the settlers, and not the other way round. But practice has shown the concept of permanent reserves to be an evil one; it can never produce equality, only the subjection of one group to another.

The Tasmanians

The story of the Tasmanians provides a concrete example of all the factors touched upon earlier in this introduction. It illustrates in classic form the fate of hundreds of other societies which fell before the advance of 'progress' and 'civilization'. It is ironic that the Tasmanians should have acquired their doubtful fame, even glamour, by becoming extinct; this feat, moreover, was achieved in recent historical times, and by a people believed to have constituted a distinct race. Within a generation the Tasmanian people were wiped out, leaving behind a handful of bones and hair, skulls, photographs, drawings and artefacts; their origins and way of life remain largely a matter for scientific conjecture.

The small size of their island and their own limited numbers meant that, considering the moral climate of the times, the total extinction of the Tasmanians was inevitable. Western cultural systems in the early nineteenth century were ethnocentric (people believed that their own race was intrinsically superior to all others). Thus arguments have been produced to show that soldiers, settlers, administrators and missionaries who caused the death of the Tasmanian people were morally guiltless. They felt no moral pressure to preserve Tasmanian culture, which died out as a result of the Tasmanians' own indifference, rather than through any white man's deliberate policy of extermination. But let their story show whether this was the case or not.

First of all, what do we know about this people and their early life on an island in the cold southern seas? We know a great deal about what they did *not* do or have. They had no clothes, no knowledge of fire-making, no domesticated animals – not even the dog – no knowledge of farming, no houses, no pots, no basketry and no methods of boiling water. It was also thought that they had no initiation rites, no moral sense and no religion. But no one bothered to study their mythology, the way they thought or their social structure – although it is clear from the complex cosmologies and social structures unearthed among equally simple peoples by modern anthropologists and ethnographers that the Tasmanians, too, must have had comparable systems and beliefs.

Some settlers, missionaries and amateur scientists did nevertheless measure the occasional head and some observation of the 'natives' was carried out, if through steadfastly European eyes. From these efforts we know that they differed from their closest neighbours, the Australians, in that they had reddish-brown skin and fuzzy hair, and that the men hunted the bush for kangaroo and wallaby and the women dived in the sea for shellfish. It is now thought that they arrived in the island about ten thousand years ago across a land bridge which then connected the island with Australia. This probably explains

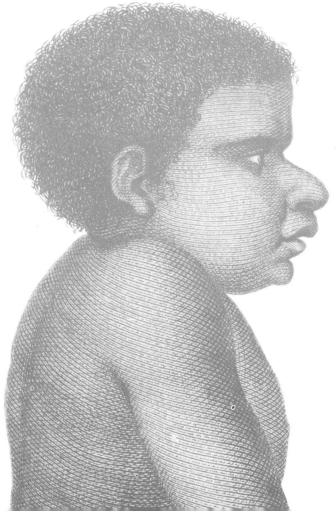

their special physical attributes: in the course of thousands of years of isolation and inbreeding local characteristics would have tended to develop. The Tasmanians were divided into different bands, each speaking different dialects of their unique language; and wars between the bands were not unknown.

The Tasmanians first saw the white man in the form of Dutch and English explorers, and a French scientific expedition. Abel Janszoon Tasman, the Dutch navigator who discovered the island for the rest of the world, arrived there in 1642 on a voyage that took him also to New Zealand and to some of the islands of Tonga and Fiji. Tasman's patron was Anton Van Diemen, a Dutch colonial administrator, and until 1853 the island was known as Van Diemen's Land. More than a century after Tasman, Captain Cook visited the island in 1777; the other important early visitor was the French naturalist Peron.

In great contrast to the reaction of later settlers, the first explorers considered the Tasmanians to be a sympathetic race: reference was made by Captain Cook to their 'benevolent expressions', their 'quick sparkling eyes' and the gentle confidence they showed in the weird white-skinned monsters who arrived in floating islands with sticks that exploded and killed without any visible human force. The sailors who landed on the Tasmanian shores must have seemed far stranger to the local inhabitants than any Martian invasion could to us, for we at least have arrived at the idea

18

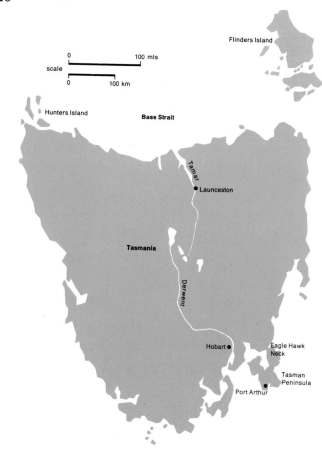

top Tasmania is 26,215 square miles in area
and situated 150 miles from the south-
east corner of Australia; its capital is Hobart.
In 1803 a British convict settlement was
established there; the island's popularity
grew as a place to farm and live, and by
1820 the white population had risen to
some 12,000; meanwhile the aborigines had
been forcibly reduced from over 2,000 to less
than 1,000; the last died in 1876.
above A group of Tasmanian aborigines.
When Captain Cook visited the island in
1777 he found their culture extremely
primitive: they had no houses or pots and
were apparently ignorant of how to make
fire or cultivate the land. Unfortunately, no
one studied their spiritual beliefs or their
social structure; now, of course, it is too late.

that other people may exist on another planet. The
Tasmanians thought the world and the universe belonged
to them; because of this it is extraordinary that they
showed the calm friendliness they did. Cook also described
the Tasmanians with sympathy; he at least thought them
'not disagreeable'.

With this in mind it is difficult to sympathize with the
attitude of the settlers who came to Tasmania from Sydney
in 1803 to establish a convict colony. For a short period the
Tasmanians showed the same friendliness they had displayed to Captain Cook and to Peron, the French naturalist;
they brought the new settlers fresh meat and water, but
their gifts were repaid by patronizing hilarity, gunfire and
sexual assault. Within a few years they had come to be
considered as little more than 'vermin' to be shot down,
just another element of island life which had to be overcome,
rather like an area of dense bush that needed to be hacked
away.

The beginning of the end came a year after the initial
settlement, when a mixed group of Tasmanians suddenly
appeared over a hill in front of a white man's camp. They
were chasing kangaroos, and they pursued them across the
area of the camp, advancing in quite large numbers
towards the stone huts and shelters of the frightened
settlers. The commander of the camp – without reason,
considering the presence of women and children in the
group – loaded his cannons with grapeshot and fired into
the mob of aborigines. Many were killed and wounded.
Appalled, the Tasmanians stopped, hesitated, then collected
their dead and wounded and retired into the bush.

Naturally enough the blacks avenged themselves on the
whites. The first case was an attack on a group of sailors
gathering oysters. It should be stressed here that on the
whole the Tasmanians murdered white men only from
motives of revenge and there is hardly one case of unpro-
voked aggression on their part. Nevertheless within twenty
years the wiping out of the natives by settler and soldier
had begun in earnest. By 1820 there were twelve thousand
settlers on the island and probably less than a thousand
aborigines. The greed for land of these farmers and graziers
was unquenchable, and they chased the original inhabitants
into wild and inhospitable land in the centre and the west.
The aborigines did not accept the alienation of their
hunting lands without protest. When they saw cattle
grazing on lands which had supported the kangaroo, they
speared the cattle. The settlers, in turn, reacted as shep-
herds do when their sheep are eaten by foxes: they shot
the aborigines.

left Convicts with pickaxes. By 1847 the island population of 70,164 included 43,730 settlers and 24,188 convicts; the remainder were military personnel and a few natives.
below A view across the Salt Pan Plain, a peaceful land that was soon to resound with the noise of hunting horns as English settlers in pink coats pursued the hapless natives.

The settlers even organized extermination parties, at which they dressed themselves in pink hunting jackets imported from England, and hunted the natives to the sound of tally-ho and the baying of hounds. In their newspaper they wrote: 'Self-defence is the first law of nature. The government must remove the natives: if not, they will be hunted down like wild beasts and destroyed.'

And so they were destroyed, with barbarous cruelty and brutality. As one contemporary historian records: 'The wounded were brained, the infants cast into the flames, the musket was driven into the quivering flesh and the social fire around which the native gathered to slumber became, before morning, their funeral pyre.' Those not killed sometimes faced a worse fate. A giant steel-jawed trap was on one occasion placed in a barrel of flour when starving aborigines were known to be in the district looking for food. Natives were flogged with cat-o'-nine-tails made of kangaroo hide or burnt with brands. Men and boys were emasculated by stockmen who wanted their women. Natives were used for target practice and their flesh thrown to the dogs. In Hobart Town a white man was given ten lashes for cutting off an aborigine's finger to use as a tobacco stopper; yet the same judge gave a convict servant fifty lashes for 'smiling at some orders given by his mistress'.

By 1830 there were only a few hundred 'wild' Tasmanians still living in the bush, although a similar number known as the 'Tame Mob' lived in the towns. These people were a sorry sight, ravaged by diseases introduced by the white man, particularly syphilis. At about this time attempts were made by the government to control the bush people or 'Wild Ones'. It was planned to restrict them to a certain part of the island, and to give them 'passports' to visit special hunting grounds. The government passed one law after another, all incomprehensible to an illiterate, starving and terror-stricken people. In one bizarre effort to improve communications picture boards were painted which colourfully depicted the problems of white-black co-existence – with pictures of whites being hanged for killing blacks and vice versa.

The Black Line

However, even such gestures were not universally approved. And in 1830 Colonel Arthur, the Governor of Tasmania, decided to remove the menace of the blacks once and for all, and a full-scale offensive was launched against the 'Wild' Tasmanians that remained. This offensive took the form of the Tasmanian Black Line, as it became known, a fantastic project which involved minutely searching every

right and below The scene at Eagle Hawk Neck. This narrow strip linked the mainland with the Tasman peninsula, where convicts were held at Port Arthur. This, too, was the target of the Black Line of 1830, an organized sweep of the island intended to herd the surviving natives on to the peninsula; but only two were captured.

above George Robinson, described at the foot of this contemporary portrait as the 'Pacificator of the Aborigines', otherwise the missionary who rounded up and accompanied 203 Tasmanians to exile on Flinders Island; there they suffered his sermons and wore the clothes he made them wear, and eventually lost the will to live.

left Part of the extraordinary proclamation of 1816 ordered by Governor Davey to teach the Tasmanians that all men, white as well as black, would be punished for any crime they committed. But not every white man agreed. The *Colonial Times* said: 'Self-defence is the first law of nature. The government must remove the natives: if not they will be hunted down like wild beasts and destroyed.'

acre of the island in order to herd the natives into the Tasman peninsula, an isthmus joined to the mainland by a narrow neck of land. This was a natural, escape-proof trap, and already harboured Van Diemen's Land's convicts.

Two thousand troops and civilians gathered. Bands played, plumes waved and all the paraphernalia of the British Army was brought to bear in order to hunt down two hundred naked, unarmed 'savages'. The hunters were spaced out in a line across the bush, and shots and bugle calls were used to maintain contact as the line marched forward. On 8 October 1830 the Black Line advanced along a 120-mile front, but within a day or two the impossibility of the plan became apparent. The shrubland was impenetrable. But the armed force struggled on, though in growing despair. The men's clothes were ripped and shredded in the bush and they were soaked by torrential rain. Meanwhile, however, the frightened aborigines passed at night behind the ranks of the Black Line; and after seventeen days of searching not one Tasmanian crossed the neck into the isthmus. During the whole expedition, only two were captured, one of whom escaped!

An Island Prison

A different and more humane scheme eventually succeeded in herding the Tasmanians together. George Robinson, a missionary from London, visited them in the bush and over the next five years persuaded most of them to surrender. In 1835 one of the last families to come in told Robinson that they had been trying to surrender for years but that each time they approached a farm they had been shot at. A so-called 'fierce tribe' which the settlers had been hunting for months also came in: these people from the 'Big River and Oyster Bay' group, were then found to number only sixteen men and boys, nine women and one child! At last, scarcely twenty years after the first settlement of the island by the English it was reported that the colony 'had the very great advantage of being free from a native population'. Although for many years groups still hung around the major towns, this assertion was very nearly true.

The rest of the 'Wild Ones' were sent to Flinders Island, off the north-east coast of Tasmania, which had been chosen as a reserve; and George Robinson was made the resident chaplain and superintendent. They arrived in the bleak island, pathetically eager to start a new life, but even as they came ashore for the first time 'they experienced the greatest agitation, gazing with strained eyes at the sterile shore, uttering melancholic moans, and with arms hanging

beside them, trembling with convulsive feeling.'

Robinson's first move was to clothe them, particularly the women who almost caused a riot among the sex-starved soldiers sent to guard them. The once proud and naked hunters then sat down to salt beef and sweet tea, dressed in duck suits, Scotch bonnets and other cast-off clothing sent out from England. In the morning they obediently watched the Union Jack being hoisted and then went to school, where the women learned washing up, baking and laundry and the men learned hygiene, table manners and how to grow strawberries. Robinson also insisted that the aborigines should learn western values, particularly market values, and they practised buying and selling interminably. As they discovered how to handle money they also learned to steal; these ways forcibly replaced the 'savage' customs of old.

Every day the Tasmanians went to church to hear Robinson's scarcely inspired sermons. One has been recorded; it went like this: 'One God. . . . One good God. . . . Native good, native dead, go up to sky. God up. . . . Bad native dead, goes down, evil spirit, fire stops. Native cry, cry, cry, . . .' And after the sermon came the catechism, when the puzzled Tasmanians obediently answered Robinson's bizarre questions:

Q: *What will God do to the world by and by?*
A: *Burn it!*
Q: *Do you like the Devil?*
A: *Noooo!*
Q: *What did God make us for?*
A: *His own purposes.*
Q: *What is the seventh day called?*
A: *Sunday.*
Q: *What is an ark?*
A: *? ?*

And at the question 'Did you know anything about God before?' it is said that there was frequently a long silence, when the Tasmanians grew sad, and sulked, and were reluctant to chant the answer 'no'.

In the few years that followed, the Tasmanians grew sadder and sadder, sulkier and sulkier. To Robinson's dismay they began to die off, while the women showed increasing signs of sterility. In addition to epidemics of colds and influenza, tuberculosis made disastrous inroads. Nor did the natives show any great will to stay alive. As their happiness diminished Robinson persisted in his attempts to interest them in his games and catechisms. By 1838, only a few years after their arrival in the island, there were only eighty-two left, all suffering from chronic influenza and chest complaints and all stricken with total apathy. In one year fifty died of pneumonia, and by 1842, given the age of all the women left, it was clear that the race was doomed.

For this state of affairs Robinson, the missionary, must be partly blamed. Everything which made life worth living for the Tasmanians was banned. They were made to feel ashamed of their own culture. They never hunted or gathered fruits and plants. Even their famous corroborees (night festivals) were prohibited; Robinson complained that 'they consisted of the most violent exercises and distortions of the body, continued to the greatest excitement and whilst in the state of violent perspiration they drank copiously of cold water, which practice was attended by the most painful results'. After the ban the 'yells and monotonous chanting' which used to disturb the Robinson family's sleep were heard no more, much to the latter's contentment since they were revelries 'which were sometimes of an obscene nature'. Despite Robinson's efforts on behalf of the aborigines and the fact that he is a culture hero of modern white Tasmanians, it would not be unfair to say that his clothes, his kindness and his unthinking Christianity killed them off more effectively than bullets. He himself prospered mightily, had two wives and reared an inordinately large family.

Finally the settlement was abandoned and the few survivors were removed to a desolate, windswept half-acre at Oyster Cove, about twenty-five miles south of Hobart, where they mouldered for a few years without Robinson's attentions – a vermin-ridden, filthy people, sleeping with a horde of mangy dogs for warmth.

Meanwhile in Tasmania a few of the 'Tame Mob' had managed to eke out an existence. Some of the last aborigines in fact achieved a certain degree of notoriety. One of them, called Mahinna, had been taken up as a young girl by a blue-stocking governor's wife, Lady Jane Franklin, who taught her civilized graces such as reading and writing, embroidery and playing the spinet. For a time she wore a crinoline and shared the life of the English ladies at Government House. However, when that governor's term of office came to an end Mahinna was left with no resources to cope with her new situation. She roamed the wharves and streets of Hobart Town, reduced to rags and begging for food. She ended up as a harlot of the timber workers at Oyster Cove and died from drowning, by then a hopeless alcoholic, a few years after her brief but successful attempt to adapt to civilization at Government House.

Grass trees on Flinders Island, the bleak land to which George Robinson's Tasmanians were transported.

left A group of the last surviving Tasmanians. Under Robinson the natives learned to wear clothes, which increased their susceptibility to fatal colds, influenza and chest complaints.
below The Flinders Island Settlement.

By the 1860s there was only one man and a few women left. 'King Billy', the last Tasmanian male, became a Hobart Town curiosity, poked at, measured, painted and photographed. He also was an alcoholic, and he died from cholera and dysentery in a tavern in 1869. His grave was robbed by local doctors and amateur scientists.

The last Tasmanian of all was called Trugannini. She became a well-known and respected figure in Hobart during her last years. She received a pension and was nicknamed 'Queen Victoria', and always wore a voluminous skirt and a red turban. Despite her pleas to be buried 'over the mountains', her skeleton was also dug up; and her remains dangled for years in a room in Hobart's museum, where it

was inspected by groups of schoolchildren and casual visitors who had come to see 'The Last of the Tasmanian Race'. Recently, following objections raised by well-meaning friends of the Tasmanians, she has been accommodated in a well-built coffin and placed in a special memorial room in the museum's basement: not to be opened except for scientific purposes. Poor Trugannini, her lifetime spanned the most critical period of contact between her people and the intrusive European settlers. She, too, had her own fair share of violence and tragedy. She had been captured by whites and watched her 'accomplices' hanged for murder. She stood helplessly by while her betrothed husband had his hands chopped off by 'civilized'

Finally the Flinders Island Settlement was abandoned and the survivors removed to a half-acre site at Oyster Cove, where they lived in squalor for a few more years. Another ragged remnant, known as the 'Tame Mob', begged a meagre living in the towns. The last Tasmanian male, 'King Billy', an alcoholic, died in 1869. His grave was robbed by local doctors and amateur scientists.

Europeans, and she saw them stab her mother to death. And yet she remained optimistic to the last, for many years acting as Robinson's mediator, helping to bring in her 'wild' compatriots from the bush before they were transported to Flinders Island. Her optimism is somehow a tribute to the qualities which her race was never given the opportunity to develop in a white-dominated island.

That, then, is the Tasmanians' story: a simple one of brutal extermination. Many may say it is best forgotten, that it happened in the past and could scarcely be repeated elsewhere, particularly in the enlightened present. We shall see that this is an over-optimistic view.

Chapter 2

LOST WORLDS

Since their extinction the Tasmanians have acquired a certain notoriety. They were an island people and their special claim to attention has probably arisen from the notion that they were a race distinct in evolutionary terms – although this was never submitted to scrutiny by the measuring instruments of the anthropologist nor to the questioning of the conscientious ethnographer. However, there is nothing unique about either the Tasmanians or the fact of their extinction. 'Cousins' of the Tasmanians have been found in northern Australia and New Guinea; and many other isolated peoples have been exterminated throughout the world and are still being exterminated. South America provides many historical and contemporary examples.

Extinction in Tierra del Fuego

The Yahgan, who formerly inhabited Tierra del Fuego, were the southernmost and traditionally the most primitive people in the world. Although they were discovered in 1624, contact with these naked fishermen who occupied the 'bottom of the world' – where the Andean *cordillera* drops into the southern seas – was not made until the eighteenth century. European sailors, battling their way around Cape Horn to enter the Pacific from the Atlantic, regularly saw smoky fires on the distant land. These were in fact lit to warn natives out in canoes that another strange winged object had been sighted out to sea, and from this early warning system came the region's name, Tierra del Fuego, meaning literally 'Fireland'.

The Yahgan inhabited no island paradise, but a bleak land of channels and fjords, drenched for most months of the year in cold rain and sleet. Two of Captain Cook's men went ashore there and froze to death in the hills – and that was in summertime! A first group of missionaries died there of cold and starvation without contacting the Yahgan. A second attempt provoked a massacre by Yahgan 'cannibals', as they were described. Finally a British ship managed to capture four of them. These four squat, short, unhandsome Yahgan then shed the small capes of sea-otter fur which they wore around their shoulders, and put on English clothes to visit the court of William IV. Three of

previous page A cluster of Yahgan wigwams made of branches, turf and grass; although the artist's 'cutaway' style exaggerates the lack of cover, it is clear that the wigwams were barely adequate for the bleak climate of Tierra del Fuego; whenever the wind changed, the ever-open doorway was moved round to the lee side.

above a painting by Alexander Buchan recording the early contact made between Yahgan tribesmen and members of Captain Cook's expedition to Tierra del Fuego in 1769. below An early drawing (1776) of a Fuegian, showing the broad, flattish features of these southerly peoples.

the four, by then known as 'York Minster', 'Fuega Basket' and 'Jimmy Button', survived to be returned to their homeland in the company of Charles Darwin aboard the survey vessel HMS *Beagle*, which set out from England in 1831. It was from these men that our first misconceptions about the Yahgan were acquired. One was that their language was as simple as their culture: Darwin thought that they had about a hundred words – yet there are some thirty-two thousand in the Yahgan dictionary, compiled later. Another concerned their cannibalism. The captive Yahgan were persistently asked if they ate men. They, seeing that the white men required an affirmative answer, gave it. Even Darwin believed the stories invented by these three. 'Meat of old woman especially good,' he was told. In fact, despite long periods of famine, they have never been known to eat human beings, not even the old people who underwent mercy-killing; instead they fought their hunger by chewing the bark of trees, leather thongs and hide moccasins.

The Yahgan lasted for two generations after the beginning of permanent contact with Europeans. The latter were not land-hungry farmers, soldiers, bush-rangers or ex-convicts, but a single family of kind-hearted Anglican missionaries who brought the comfort of God and clothes to the 'benighted' Yahgan in the 1860s. How was it, then, that this simple people could have survived a miserably cold climate and harsh environment for over a thousand years, only to succumb in a few years to the kindly attentions of the European?

Three thousand Yahgan, a race of shore- and crag-dwellers, were scattered along miles of rocky coastline, subsisting on shellfish, sea-mammals and birds. Even in the worst weather the women paddled their canoes around the inlets, and dived into the icy waters, often with babies on their backs; the babies at such times climbed to safety on the women's heads, where they could also avoid the cold and prickly kelp. The men hunted sea-mammals or hauled ashore the occasional stranded whale; the blubber was stored underground for leaner months. They also gathered fuel for their essential fires, collected fungi and caught cormorants, geese and – at night – swans, which they hunted with the aid of torches, rushing at the roosting birds and clubbing them to death. The material culture necessary for such a simple livelihood was of the simplest kind and their inventory of tools, weapons and other gear was limited, in effect, to bare essentials.

We know quite a lot about the Yahgan from the detailed and sympathetic accounts written by the English missionary family, the Bridges, who observed the people as they

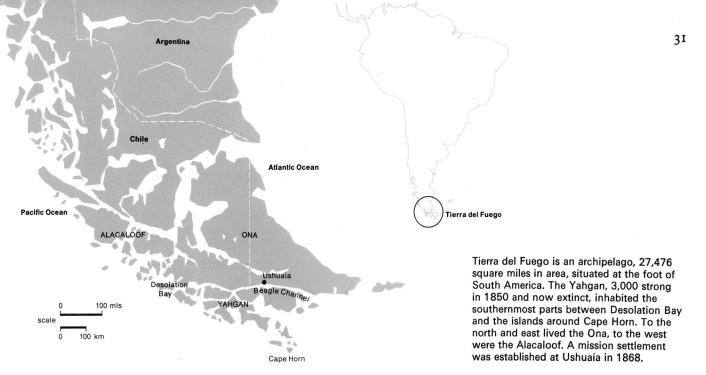

Tierra del Fuego is an archipelago, 27,476 square miles in area, situated at the foot of South America. The Yahgan, 3,000 strong in 1850 and now extinct, inhabited the southernmost parts between Desolation Bay and the islands around Cape Horn. To the north and east lived the Ona, to the west were the Alacaloof. A mission settlement was established at Ushuaia in 1868.

right Ona Indians, members of a hunting tribe that in more primitive days relied heavily for food and clothing on the guanaco, a kind of llama. **below** Ona tribesmen outside their *hain,* a secret lodge from which all women were banned; the painted man is impersonating a creature from Ona mythology.

constantly moved about from beach to beach, and from one temporary settlement to another. We have elaborate descriptions of their wigwams, their fishing techniques, their dances and their art; and it is to the Bridges that we owe our knowledge of the Yahgan language. Yet despite the obvious sympathy of the straight-laced though good-humoured and constant missionaries for their native friends, the Bridges were convinced that the Yahgan lacked any idea of God. They described in great detail their initiation and wedding ceremonies, but nowhere indicated that these contained religious elements. To most people the Fuegians were cannibals; and the missionaries – who should have known better – were determined to believe that they had no god. Wedding feasts were seen as merely parties. A person's death was not the occasion for a religious rite, but an excuse for the Yahgan to paint their bodies and gash their breasts with sharp stones. Their myths were called fairy stories and their initiation rites were seen as youthful games.

Fortunately the Yahgan were also studied by an anthropologist who, whatever his own blind-spots, did not believe that only Protestant Christians had access to the benefits of religion. We now know that their god played an important part in Fuegian marriage, funeral and initiation rites and entered into all their thoughts, emotional life and personal behaviour. They had priests, or shamans, who assigned individual guardian spirits to all babies. They had a very definite belief in a supreme being, whom they called 'Master' or 'Ruler', who gave life, took it away and inflicted supernatural punishment if a Yahgan broke one of the religious taboos. And their 'fairy stories' were in reality part of a complex body of Yahgan cosmology that even included an indigenous Flood story.

The missionaries did not try to convert the natives as aggressively and stubbornly as George Robinson in Tasmania and it must have seemed likely that the Yahgan – without the curse of European settlers on their territory – might remain undisturbed in their cold and gloomy lands. Unfortunately they did not have a chance to survive. In 1884 their population was still roughly three thousand; in that year Argentina set up a sub-prefecture in the region (their southernmost territory) and sent twenty men to administer it. The Yahgan were friendly and allowed six of their boys and one man to go aboard the Argentinian ship; within hours they and their friends and relatives were struck down with a strange illness.

Soon the Yahgan were dying at such a rate that the missionaries and an Argentinian doctor could do nothing for them. The latter diagnosed the illness as typhoid pneumonia. Whole families died; babies were left unattended and starving in their huts. In outlying settlements they died in such numbers that the dead were dragged to the nearest bushes or, if their relatives lacked the strength to move them even that far, they were left outside their wigwams. Near the mission thirty children died despite the missionary's wife's attempts to save them: it was her diagnosis of the illness that proved correct in the end: it was a bout of measles. It wiped out half the population of one Yahgan district and left the survivors so reduced in vitality that fifty per cent of these survivors succumbed in the next two years.

Everyone was appalled by this sudden disaster. The Yahgan, who had proved themselves so strong in the face of their bleak climate and unrewarding environment, who recovered incredibly quickly from vicious hunting wounds and sprains, had collapsed before a childish ailment. Nevertheless, childish or not, it marked the beginning of the end for the Yahgan. After the first epidemic they were reduced from three thousand to one thousand. In 1899 they numbered two hundred; in 1902, a hundred and thirty; in 1913 there were less than a hundred. In 1933, the last time a 'census' was taken, forty remained and today they are 'presumed extinct'. After measles there was typhoid, whooping cough, smallpox and respiratory diseases. Other factors which contributed to their fall included changes in their diet, and the introduction of clothing and alcohol.

Brazil

A century after the Yahgan's first fatal encounter with the white man people on the same continent are still suffering the same kind of fate. In considering the plight of the Brazilian Indian today, we should bear in mind the details of what happened to the Tasmanians and the Yahgan, since the events that led to their extinction are being repeated almost exactly in central Brazil. There the Indians are in the news today primarily because they are the last of Latin America's tribes to have avoided assimilation or extermination.

The story of the Indians' decimation in Brazil is long and unremitting. It began with the first days of European exploration and settlement, when soldiers – acting on instructions from Portugal – massacred all Indians on sight. The soldiers added their own refinements to this brutal commission by hanging Indians by their feet, ripping them apart with horses or canoes, burying them alive or leaving

below South America was opened up by the Spanish and Portuguese in the late fifteenth century. Thousands of native Indians were shot, tortured and dismembered by the invaders; in return they devised suitable punishments for their European captives, such as forcing them to swallow, in molten form, quantities of the gold after which they had lusted.

them to be eaten alive by ants. Meanwhile in Portugal learned Christian doctors endlessly argued whether these anthropoids in feather headdresses had souls or not; in the end the Pope solemnly declared that they had.

The Europeans conquered Brazil, exterminating, driving back or assimilating the Indian, expropriating his land and working it themselves or with imported slave-labour. Those who managed to slip through the net of the European advance survived until the nineteenth century, when a world-wide demand for rubber opened the Amazon Basin to international commerce and led many of the Indians to give up their traditional way of life to collect rubber. During this phase of contact with the white man large num-

bers of Indians died from malnutrition, the result of their unaccustomed diet of dried beans and tinned food, and from epidemics of new illnesses and social diseases such as gonorrhoea and syphilis. Faced with these new scourges the Indians once again fled the advance of civilization and retired to a further hundred years of peace in the forests and plains of places like the Mato Grosso, a remote and thinly populated region of Brazil's south-western plateau.

Unfortunately the campaign against the Indians has escalated in the last few years. This is because the land of the few remaining Indian tribes is to be developed by the Brazilian government for the benefit of its millions of inhabitants who are below the poverty line. A modern

34

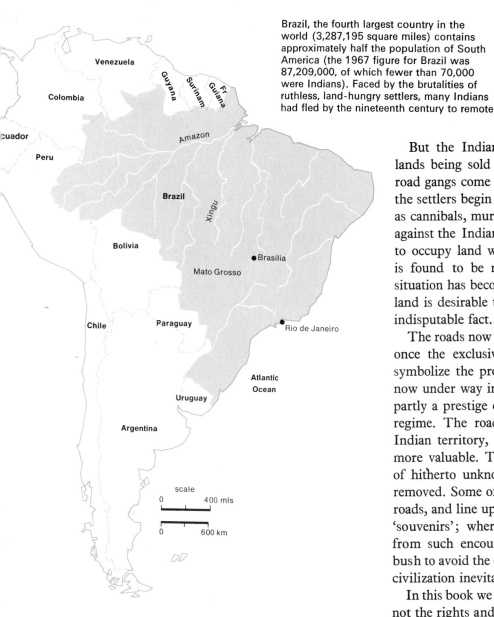

Brazil, the fourth largest country in the world (3,287,195 square miles) contains approximately half the population of South America (the 1967 figure for Brazil was 87,209,000, of which fewer than 70,000 were Indians). Faced by the brutalities of ruthless, land-hungry settlers, many Indians had fled by the nineteenth century to remote regions like the Mato Grosso in the south-west. Today Indian land is once more in demand and the threat of extermination for these disturbed peoples is greater than ever.

But the Indians are the problem. Not only are their lands being sold off, but they have to be pacified before road gangs come in, and then removed to new land before the settlers begin farming, since they are universally feared as cannibals, murderers and headshrinkers. This campaign against the Indians is not new, but now that they turn out to occupy land which is considered valuable farmland or is found to be rich in minerals and rare metals, their situation has become even more precarious. In areas where land is desirable the Indian population dies off: this is an indisputable fact.

The roads now cutting through huge territories that were once the exclusive preserve of a few thousand Indians symbolize the problem. The massive road-building effort now under way in the Amazon Basin and central Brazil is partly a prestige effort on the part of the present military regime. The roads are creeping resolutely forward into Indian territory, making the surrounding land more and more valuable. They are passing through the homelands of hitherto unknown tribes that have to be pacified and removed. Some of these peoples are fatally attracted to the roads, and line up beside them to sell their pathetic tourist 'souvenirs'; whereas others have already suffered badly from such encounters and have retired further into the bush to avoid the epidemics and despair which contact with civilization inevitably brings.

In this book we are concerned with the fate of the Indians, not the rights and wrongs of road-building or the exploitation of the jungle for the benefit of rich foreigners or poor Brazilians. The Indians, once numbered in millions, now total less than seventy thousand; they range from a few thoroughly integrated groups in the south of the country to completely isolated peoples in the Amazon region. The survival of the latter has become a matter of great concern: if nothing is done they will all be exterminated or die off in a few years. Their extinction will not be as the result of any official, systematic plan for their destruction by a hostile government; talk of genocide smacks of sensationalism. The Indians are dying off because there is such a lack of understanding of their predicament. Add to this a paucity of funds, a general indifference and, most of all, the state of savagery and lawlessness which exists in Brazil's unpoliced frontierlands, and a fuller though still depressing picture emerges.

It may seem surprising, but in fact the laws of Brazil have been favourable to the Indian for a long time. The government recognized early on that the Indians would have to be protected and the Indian Protection Service was

frontier-feeling is abroad in Brazil; as new lands are opened up for farmers and cattle-raisers there is a mood of fresh optimism. The more fertile areas are carved into plots of from ten to one hundred acres and the overcrowded poor of north-eastern Brazil are being encouraged to take up concessions there.

Most of the land is unsuitable for smallholdings, however, and many of the pioneers fail after one or two years and then cannot even manage to find their fares home. Consequently, instead of the land being opened up to the poor it is merely being exploited by the rich – by foreign landholders, road haulage contractors and land speculators. One fifth of Brazil is owned by foreigners, most of them Americans; rich proprietors are being allocated vast stretches of land in the Mato Grosso and other areas at a minimal price on condition that the land is fenced and divided among peasant labour from the north-east. But the peasants usually remain as poor as they were before; any profits go to the big operators who open up the land and then watch its value increase.

below Imported negro slave labour washing for diamonds, another facet of white domination in Brazil. Many Indians who survived similar treatment in, for example, the rubber trade in the Amazon Basin, withdrew into the jungle, preferring the dangers of occasional brushes with roving bands of Portuguese (**bottom**) to the miseries of assimilation.

founded in 1911. Unfortunately it did not achieve what it set out to do – to prevent a repetition of atrocities committed against the Indians by adventurers and settlers who had butchered whole tribes or flogged, tortured and starved Indian workers who had stepped out of line.

The Brazilian government itself has published a report which revealed the scope of the carnage against the Indian in recent years, implicating senior Indian Service officials who had taken advantage of their position to make fortunes from Indian lands. Others were accused of murdering or terrorizing Indians in order to force them off their territory, and one former director of the Service was said to have committed forty-two crimes against the local people including collusion in several murders, torture and the illegal sale of land. His profits amounted to more than £300,000. Another official was accused of embezzlement and other misuses of Indian Service funds, and of torturing and enslaving dozens of Indians. Whole tribes were killed off in Bahia State. In 1962 a gift of sugar to a community was seasoned with arsenic and conveniently wiped out the

Tapaiuna Indians, while another Mato Grosso tribe was shot up by a band of gunmen who then bombed them from the air with 'bananas' – a Brazilian slang term for sticks of dynamite.

The story of the death of Indian peoples and their cultures – part of a 'civilizing' process in which the last virgin areas of the world are being consumed – is one of appalling tragedy that easily lends itself to sensationalism and a reiteration of the atrocities of man against man. These few examples already mentioned, which were taken from an official report, will suffice. What is more important in a situation where harassment and murder is so widespread is to discuss what can be done for the Indian both by the new Indian Service, the Fundaçaõ Naçional do Indio (whose work is still hindered by stifling policies, lack of funds, and graft) and by outside agencies such as charitable institutions and missions.

The Indians of the Mato Grosso

First of all, who are these Indians? We are familiar with newspaper pictures of naked men, a little out of focus, who appear to be aiming blows or brandishing clubs at bold, intrepid journalists in their flying machines. We have seen in travel books and glossy magazines the painted patterns on their faces and bodies, their blowpipes and poisoned arrows, and examples of their headshrinking techniques. And their elaborate cosmologies have received a good deal of publicity recently in the anthropo-philosophical debates waged between Claude Lévi-Strauss and Jean-Paul Sartre, and in the current rage for 'structuralism'. (The latter, very broadly, implies that culture and social organization are based on a kind of logical groundplan discernible through study of particular groups and societies.) Let us now look a little more closely at some of these peoples.

The Mato Grosso, perhaps the most mysterious and romantic region of the world, is primarily flat savannah, barely rising out of water, turned by floods into mud bogs and marshes. It is a vast land once inhabited by hundreds of small tribes, each with its own culture and language, each usually at loggerheads with its neighbours. One of the best known tribes is the Nambikwara. The name in fact covers a group of tribes scattered over an area half the size of France; they formed the sparsest population of South America and probably had the simplest technology, pursuing a semi-nomadic life collecting wild plants, animals and fish.

The Nambikwara have always had a reputation for ferocity. In the early years of the twentieth century they became known as the 'Wooden Muzzles' because of the wooden discs they wore in their lower lips and the lobes of their ears. They were conspicuously avoided by Europeans after they had invited a party of seven to visit them in 1925, who were never heard of again. In the 1930s Protestant missionaries moved in, but relations never

became very cordial, primarily, it is said, because the Nambikwara were not pleased with their gifts. Then one day, when an Indian arrived at the dispensary with fever, he was given two aspirins, went swimming to cool himself and then dropped dead, almost at once, in front of his friends. To the Nambikwara, who were themselves expert poisoners, it was clear that he had been poisoned, and six members of the mission, including a baby of two, were massacred, leaving one woman alive to tell the story. The incident naturally increased hostility among outsiders.

The Nambikwara belong to a physical type which differentiates them from most other tribes and links them to an ancient race whose bones have been found in Brazil. Their only clothing is a tuft of straw that the men wear above the penis; the men are usually five feet tall and the women three inches shorter; their skins are darker than other Indians', and they have more body-hair and longer heads. Their year follows a clear pattern: in the wet season each band takes up temporary lodgings on a slope overlooking a river bed, and there they erect their rough and ready shelters, which are made so that they can be moved around during the day to protect them from the sun. The men split up into small roving bands to search for game while the women scour the jungle for grubs, spiders, grasshoppers, rodents, snakes, lizards, fruit, seeds, roots and honey. They come together in quite large groups for ceremonial and festive occasions or to defend themselves

from witchcraft attack or the aggression of their neighbours.

At present the Nambikwara are being squeezed out by farmers, land speculators and diamond-seekers. From twenty thousand their population has sunk to the dramatically low figure of seven hundred. A few have not been contacted, but most have been herded into villages, and two hundred live in a reserve of their own. However, they are occupying desirable land and so they live in constant fear of being chased off their lands or shot. Their reserves have no facilities, they are not taught farming methods, game stocks have been exhausted and in many cases communities of Nambikwara who are sworn and deadly enemies are being placed in neighbouring villages. But for the protection of a few young anthropologists and missionaries we should be writing of them in the past tense today.

Decline of the Bororo

Many other Mato Grosso peoples, such as the Shavante, Sherente and Bororo lived in large settled villages and had a far more complex social structure than the Nambikwara. A Bororo village, for example, contained several hundred people living in houses which were veritable palaces; these were not built, but knotted, plaited, woven and embroidered together. Bororo villages were built in concentric circles around a central clearing with a large oval house in the middle, some sixty feet long and twenty feet wide, in which all the men lived when they were not hunting. The men's

left At the turn of the century a white diamond seeker poses with his Bororo guides. **right** A Brazilian dignitary visits a settlement of the Nambikwara, a Mato Grosso tribe once 20,000 strong, now reduced to 700.

house was the centre of both the village and of the Bororo universe, providing the focus of the relationship between society and the supernatural, the living and the dead.

The Bororo had a grandiose cosmology which can be seen in the layout of their village and the distribution of their homes. All villages were divided into two halves, or moieties; and within a village all the houses were grouped according to the moiety arrangements of the inhabitants. The moieties were known as 'Weak' and 'Strong' and were in turn divided into roughly six clans; while in some villages the Weak and Strong moieties were further divided by countervailing moieties known as Upstream and Downstream. All the men of the village were also divided into two teams and on ceremonial occasions they held races in which a two-hundred-pound tree-trunk was passed from shoulder to shoulder.

Individual houses in a Bororo village were built by men and owned according to matrilineal principles, which means that they were owned by the women of several families linked through a matrilineal connection (kinship traced through the mother). In each house a nuclear family had its fireplace and platform beds. Their material culture, while simple, was beautifully executed, and many of the women owned caskets of exquisite jewellery which passed from mother to daughter. Men were allowed to pluck out their women's hair and weave it into long ropes which they wore around their heads like a turban. They loved display, ornamentation, singing and dancing and spent hours making each other beautiful. Finally, the Bororo were deeply religious and had a complex system of beliefs and myths.

Usually anthropologists write in what is known as the 'ethnographic present'. The natives 'do' and 'make' that and 'believe' this. For the Nambikwara and the Bororo this is an inappropriate usage since they and dozens of neighbouring tribes have virtually disappeared from the face of the earth. The Bororo, through illness and indiscriminate contact with *civilizados* have been reduced within a generation to a few score, and to all intents and purposes are extinct. A few remaining Bororo live in dismal hovels made of interwoven saplings and thatch, the interiors littered with rubbish – a far cry from their old, elaborate houses.

This aerial view of an Indian village shows the special importance of the long hut in the centre of the clearing. Among the Bororo, a tragically depleted people from the Mato Grosso, the long hut was a focal point of great spiritual significance. This pattern was deliberately destroyed by missionaries as part of their quest for souls.

They wear uncomfortable and dirty clothes. They have forgotten their customs and show no interest in their traditional crafts. One or two old men try aiming their bows and arrows or stumble through half-forgotten dances for tourists, but on the whole they have become a dull and listless group, inspired only by drink and the chance of a few coins.

The Bororo have been strongly influenced by the Catholic missions, whose main efforts have been directed at the children. The missionaries learnt one very clever trick in this process of acculturation or assimilation. They soon found that the Bororo's concentric villages were essential to their social and religious life, so they made them build square huts which were lined up in parallel rows. As a result their patterns of life were disturbed, they became disorientated and all feeling for tradition left them. Perhaps, though, the effort to win Bororo souls has been a waste of time since they are now slipping rapidly to extinction.

What Is Being Done?

The Brazilian government plans to bring the Indians into Brazilian society. Some have been assimilated and have settled beside hospitals, towns and outposts where they get what work they can, although their wages are low and they must pay normal, unsubsidized prices for food. Others live in reserves where settlers have taken root; the latter pay a miniscule rent to the Indians who theoretically own the land. The Indian villages are controlled by Indian Guards, young men taken from the tribes who were educated and returned to their homes to act as a kind of native police. In many of these areas there is no work; total lethargy and depression has resulted from the Indians' enforced settlement. Nothing of value has been given them to replace the

left An Indian learns the art of brick-laying at a mission settlement. **top** In the mission school Indian children face the baffling task of learning to read and write not only in their own language but in Portuguese as well. Many missions do excellent work but tend to ignore the Indians' more pressing needs in favour of religious instruction.

left A Nambikwara family photographed
c. 1938 by the famous French anthropologist
Claude Levi-Strauss. Today the Nambikwara
are being squeezed by white expansion in
the Mato Grosso. below A Txukahamal
group in their jungle camp. Even the
remotest tribes are living on borrowed time,
their territories marked off as land lots for
new settlers.

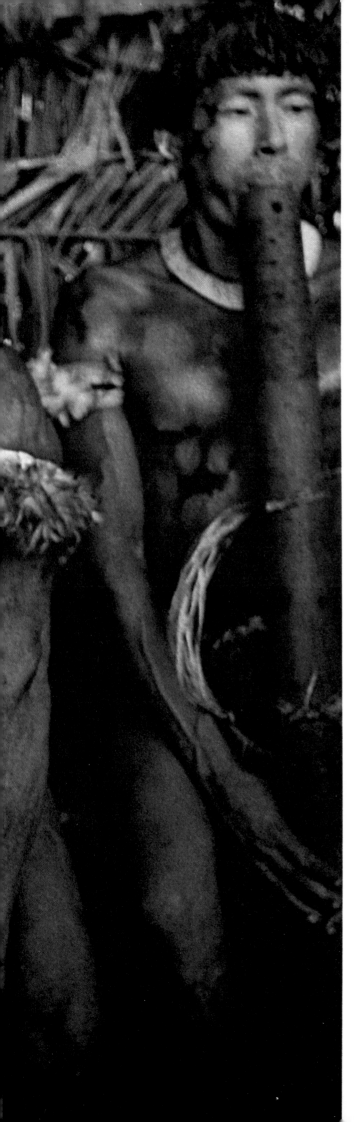

Kamaiura flute players in the Xingu National Park, a protected area run by the Villas Boas brothers in which some 1,500 Indians are being slowly acclimatized to the modern world. The musicians are praying for the rainy season to end so that they can take up their fishing again. 'We speak to our gods,' they say, 'with the sweet music of flutes.'

destruction of their former culture. Some tribes are in an appalling state: one group, the Gaviao, were put into rough shelters in a reserve and a few weeks after they had first been contacted were suffering from hacking coughs and colds, sitting dejectedly about on the ground. Other tribes are still to be contacted and they roam the forests, hostile and frightened, living in areas which have already been marked off as future land lots.

In most cases the sole protectors of the Indians are the missionaries, whose success in this role is not always conspicuous. While some groups of Indians flourish with high birth rates in communities organized by the Salesian missionaries, others are suffering from the fanaticism of do-gooders who are concerned primarily with passing on the message of the Bible. Among most Protestant Evangelical missionaries the communication of the Gospel to the Indians is the core of their missionary effort. Californian-based Wycliffe Bible translators carry to imaginative lengths the commandment to impart the Bible. They train in primitive conditions in test villages in Mexico and live unaided in the Brazilian bush for a month or two before they are dropped in by aeroplane, with their transmitters and refrigerators, among pagan Indians such as the Nambikwara and Bororo. The stubborn belief persists in many missionaries that 'salvation' is impossible or at least extremely difficult without a faith in Jesus Christ, and they aggressively oppose liberal Protestant and Catholic missionaries who are providing hospitals and education before Bible classes and hymn singing.

The rapid and recent deterioration of the Indians is credited by most anthropologists and alert observers to the blind attitudes of the missionaries, even though it is admitted that many do marvellous work. They work on simple premises: that the Christian God is the only true God and that all non-Christian beliefs are absolutely wrong and evil, and inspired (of course) by Satan. Unfortunately for the Indian, missionaries are usually the only channel through which western life is perceived.

Xingu Park and the Villas Boas Brothers

Everyone is agreed that the Indians, if they are to survive, must not be brought too quickly into contact with the wider Brazilian culture. In the process of their eventual integration it is obviously important to prevent further decimation through illness and to protect them from cultural degradation. A limited number of Brazil's Indians have the great good fortune to live in the huge protected Xingu Park, which is administered by the Villas Boas brothers.

44

A threat to the security of the Xingu Park is posed by a new road, part of the Trans-Amazonica plan to open up the whole of southern Amazonia; originally planned to pass round the Park, the road was then driven through the centre. In the map Leonardo and Diauarum are the names of the two camps run by the Villas Boas brothers.

Xingu is a national park of about 22,500 square kilometres in which there live approximately 1,500 Indians from fifteen tribes. The two Boas brothers are the two surviving members of a trio who set out a generation ago from the city of São Paulo and succeeded in establishing this reserve in the heart of Brazil; into it they have put remnants of hard-pressed Indian tribes who are then allowed to live according to their own ways, protected more or less successfully from the outside world. For almost thirty years the Boas brothers have worked in the heartland of southern Amazonia and the development of the region has depended on their trails and the airstrips that they have built. Claudio, one of the two brothers, did

not leave the jungle at one period for nine years. They have become famous among the Indians, many of whom originally went out of curiosity to see them and take advantage of their hospitality.

During this period the tribes of the Upper Xingu were in a sorry plight because their land was being alienated and bands of surveyors, prospectors and skin collectors, armed with rifles and sub-machine guns, roamed the waterways and were prepared to shoot any Indians who opposed them. But in 1961 the jungle was declared a national park, land sales were invalidated and the Boas brothers were given the authority to expel surveyors and prospectors.

The Xingu experiment has been an outstanding success.

Claudio Villas Boas takes the temperature of one of the Xingu Indians. The experiment has been a great success in that the Indians living there can retain their cultural identity and at the same time receive medical and economic aid while they adjust to their new surroundings.

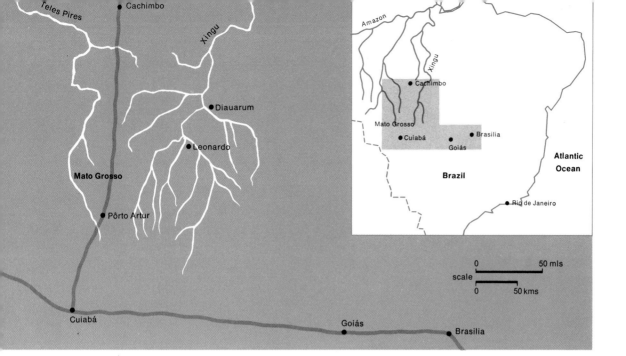

The Indian population is rising and most people are now convinced that the Boas methods have shown how the Indians of Brazil can be blended successfully into the modern world. Their plan includes a period of acclimatization for the Indian in which he is protected from the full shock of civilization. This is followed by a stage in which he adapts to the modern way of life at his own speed and according to his own needs.

It has not all been plain sailing. It can take up to two years to bring in a people who are fearful of contacting their protectors, since all they may know of the *civilizados* is the shattering noise of aeroplanes and sometimes that of gunfire. One tribe, the Txikao, which once numbered over four hundred, were down to fifty-three before Boas could contact them. They had suffered from an invasion by more than a thousand diamond-seekers, who had come down the Jajoba river, followed by federal police who were there to prevent diamond smuggling. A road had been opened and it became imperative to transfer this hungry, frightened and dispirited people to the Xingu Park. They themselves were eager to make the change but it took weeks to collect the scattered groups together.

In July 1967 fifty-three Txikao, with their bundles and pet birds, went aboard a barge of the Brazilian Air Force and travelled slowly towards the reserve. Time was allowed for hunting and fishing and bathing. Once, when they passed the hunting ground of their old enemies, they flung off their clothes, grabbed their bows and arrows and prepared to do battle. Nevertheless they arrived safe and sound at Posto Leonardo, one of the Park's main camps, and the Indians who were already settled there came to meet them, presenting them with manioc plantations, an old village, and offers of their friendship. At the same time, to the dismay of the Boas brothers, a plane-load of *civilizados* arrived to see the 'primitives' being brought in from the jungle; within a few days the whole community of new arrivals was at death's door from the germs of influenza and pneumonia left by the sensation-seekers. With prompt medical attention, however, they all survived except one.

For the people living there Xingu has proved a wonderfully successful experiment. The villagers are fit and

Tranquillity in a Xingu village. In the safety of the Park, unmolested by profiteers, the Indians have begun to fight the threat of extinction; morale has risen and their numbers are now on the increase for the first time in several generations.

top This tribesman is one of the fifty-three surviving members of the Txikao who were brought to the safety of the Xingu National Park in 1967 following a massacre by diamond prospectors. above For the Indians of Xingu, visiting aircraft bring help and encouragement of a kind rarely found outside the Park.

cheerful, still perform their dances and ceremonies, play their flutes and make pots. Some, like the Txikao, who were on the point of extinction, are now increasing. Clothes are available against cold and mosquito attacks but the Indians are not forced to wear them. Yet they are slowly changing. One interesting fact is that the cultures of the very different tribes of Xingu Park are becoming one. Although they speak separate languages and preserve their own myths, the cultures have all tended to become similar through contact.

The Park is a success. But what of the Indians outside? Xingu can take only twice its present number of Indians and there are this number of uncontacted Indians in the immediate area of the Park alone. Moreover despite its success the Park's very existence is now in danger. The Cuiabá–Cachimbo road (the BR–80), which was originally planned to pass outside the northern limits of the Park through open country, has been diverted to take a new and more difficult route through the centre of the reserve. This is a serious threat to the people whose survival involves their insulation from outside influences. Many people suspect that what is really involved is the opening up of the Upper Xingu to the developers – particularly since many politicians have already declared that the exploitation of the virgin jungle is more important than the fate of a few 'savages'. One official has said that the existence of the Park is 'prejudicial to the security and development of the country'. The Indian, he continued, along with the slum-dwellers, the hippy and all other marginal persons, should be forcibly integrated into the mainstream of society.

left The new road pierces the Xingu Park.
Its construction illuminates the inconsistency
of the Brazilian government in its handling
of the Indian problem : enlightened one year,
it allocates funds ; the next year it appears to
find its Indians an embarrassment, and their
needs are brushed aside.

above The degraded world of those
Indians who are compelled with little or no
understanding to come to terms with white
civilization, going to live either in an urban
slum or the comparable squalor of a
government reserve. In such surroundings
depression, disease and premature death are
almost inevitable.

THE LANDEATERS

Land, or at least the desire for new land, was a major factor in the extermination of the Tasmanians and of the innumerable extinct peoples of South America. In both these countries, strangers with superior farming techniques found a sparsely settled land of good resources, inhabited by weak and divided peoples. The land of the primitives was invaded by the new farmers, who also brought their plants, their animals, their illnesses and their pests.

The process is always the same: the invaders begin at the sea, moving across whole continents and islands, removing forests with their steel axes, replacing the original inhabitants' game-preserves with farmland, pasture-land, and in many cases with waste land. As the land is consumed the natives are pushed further and further towards less attractive pockets of the country. It is a swift business, since the invader is always armed with superior techniques, superior arms and an unquenchable thirst for fresh land to exploit. Scattered populations of farmers and hunters, and even the citizens of highly developed civilizations like the Maya and Inca, fall before the fur-trapper, the sealer, the cattle-raiser, the pioneer farmer and a host of miners, soldiers, explorers, missionaries and land-speculators.

At the time of Columbus and the dawning of the Age of Discovery towards the end of the fifteenth century, mankind in Europe gained access to unheard of opportunities to exploit new lands. However, in considering how he profited from these opportunities we should not, of course, forget that the exploitation of land and the extermination of its first inhabitants were not new ideas, nor were they the prerogative of Europeans in the New World. In Africa, more than a thousand years before the discovery of America by the white man, Bantu farmers invaded the equatorial forests, then inhabited solely by Pygmy and Bushmen hunters, and pushed the latter further and further back until they were confined to distant corners of the forest and to harsh, unproductive desert areas. In Asia too, Russian pioneers in the seventeenth century moved eastward into the relatively unexploited wastes of Siberia; and later, between 1861 (when serfdom was abolished) and 1914 over five million Caucasian Slavs invaded Siberia, assimilating the heterogeneous cultures that lived there.

previous page The signing of William
Penn's treaty, concluded in 1682
with the Delaware Indians of North
America. It was popularly claimed to have
been made 'without an Oath and never
broken'. In reality the agreement lasted only
during Penn's lifetime; after his death in
1718 the Delawares were soon parted from
their fertile lands.

Nor were the conflicts in which 'civilized' white Europeans took part directed only against the barbarian black or redskin. The English, for example, before their incursions upon the American Indian and the Australian aborigine, had learned to expropriate land and exterminate natives in the Celtic regions of Britain.

Civilized English and Primitive Celt

When James VI of Scotland succeeded Queen Elizabeth I on the throne of England in 1603, efforts were already being made to subjugate the 'wild men' in the Celtic lands of Scotland and Ireland. The new king, known to the English as James I, had begun his efforts with the Celtic-speaking peoples of the Hebrides, a group of islands off the west coast of Scotland. He had even given a charter to the first colonizing corporation. This was designed to take over the Celts' lands and do for a large section of Celtic Scotland what the Virginia Company was later to do in North America. In their undeveloped state the Celtic lands offered a foothold for foreign invasion; moreover they constituted a vast waste which could be filled with loyal and 'civilized' subjects from England. They, James saw, would increase the country's wealth and improve her defences. But his greed for land was, of course, the prime motive; the possibilities that the lands of the Celts offered for development, especially with the new techniques then being developed in England, were enormous. Furthermore

above James I of England (1566–1625),
whose greed for land led him to try and
exterminate the 'wild men' of the Hebrides
and other parts of Celtic Scotland with the
aim of replacing them with loyal and
'civilized' subjects from England. below
An Italian artist's view of Scottish tribemen
at the beginning of the seventeenth century.

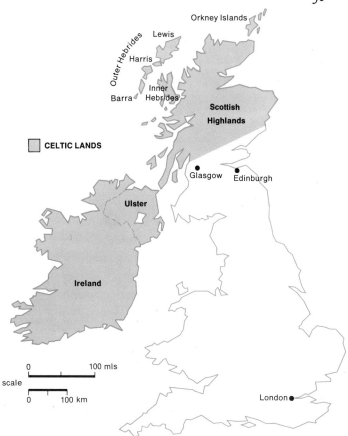

right When James I came to the throne of England in 1603 he was already King of Scotland. Even so, he had almost no control over the vast Celtic lands, which amounted to half the area of the British Isles and in their undeveloped state offered potentially dangerous footholds for any foreign power with territorial ambitions.

the Celts possessed territories which amounted to fifty per cent of the British Isles, while their population had only one-seventh the density of England's.

James justified his oppression of the Scots, and later the Irish, on the grounds that they were primitive. The wild Celts were held to be on a par with the American Indians: they were to be pacified, moved into reservations or exterminated, and their lands put to a civilized use by a civilized people. Of course, the Celts *were* as primitive as the American Indians. Although agriculture and cattle-raising were known, they were practised only on a crude level: the Celts required, for example, five men to handle a horse and plough. Politically too they were primitive. In about the year 1600 the Celtic-speaking tribes which were free of all subjection to the crowns of Scotland and England held virtually all Ireland and all the Scottish Highlands and islands. The Scottish clans and Irish *tuaths* (petty chiefdoms) were merely tribes, like typical Indian or African tribes. The clan chief was a petty prince, lord of all he surveyed, and each one was at war with his neighbours.

Politically the Celts were about on a level with the Indian chiefdoms and federations of North America; and they were of course inferior to those of Peru and Mexico and some African states. However, they were not 'niggers' or 'redskins', but as white, if not whiter, than the English. Most of the Irish and Scottish peoples were of Nordic blood, despite their Celtic speech, and the Scottish Hebrideans were almost pure Scandinavians. In the history of land expropriation in Britain the racial argument could not be used: instead the ruling body made do with the notion that a campaign was to be fought on behalf of civilization against the primitive menace.

Suppression of the Highlands

King James began his subjugation of the Highlands by giving joint stock companies title to clan lands, particularly those of the Camerons of Lochiel, the MacDonalds of Glenelg and the MacLeods of Harris. Another was given title to the largest of the Hebridean territories, Lewis. All the natives became outlaws, and the companies, which planned to make their profits from real estate development, were given the right to make war on rebels and destroy them. In Lewis the company had six hundred hired soldiers; they were not needed at first since one chief, Neill, made terms with the invaders, who were lulled into a sense of security. Then in 1600 Neill and his tribesmen massacred the colonists, killing sixty, destroying the new town and clearing the islands. King James's revenge was to import

a 'tame' barbarian tribe, the MacKenzies, whose seven hundred swordsmen soon crushed the rebel Lewis men.

This experience persuaded James to plan a general extermination of the inhabitants of the whole Highland area and he wrote to his Privy Council: 'You are to enjoin the said Marquis [in charge of the colonization] that, anent the extirpation of the barbarous people in these bounds, that he specially undertake and bind himself to extirpate and rout out the chief of Clan Ranald and his whole clan [the mainland MacDonalds] and their followers within the Isles . . . and also the MacNiel of Barra with his clan, and the whole Danald clan in the north. . . . And that he end not his service by agreement with the country people [i.e. the natives] but by extirpation of them.' Fortunately James lacked the funds to carry out his plans and instead he turned his attention to Ulster where the less wild Irish were to be put into reservations and not exterminated, as Elizabeth's councillors had originally planned. In Ulster plantation schemes were introduced and 'natives' were ordered to leave the country or enter the reserves. An order was sent out stating that any found outside the reserves after a certain date were to be executed.

Outside Ulster, the tribes remained tribal and barbarian until they were subjugated in 1649–50 by Oliver Cromwell, who sent his army into Ireland with orders to wipe out the tribal system and also the existing religious practices. Civilization in the form of English culture and the Protestant religion came to Ireland at a terrible cost. Eighty thousand natives and more were shipped to the West Indies as chattel slaves, where they toiled alongside African Negroes, and American Indians who had been shipped abroad by the Puritans of New England. Of the Irish population at home, it has been estimated that almost a million died by the sword and by starvation.

left A Dutch interpretation of the Irish of James I's period, after he had introduced plantation settlements in Ulster and installed Scottish Protestant settlers to run them; here, left to right, are a noblewoman, a middle-class woman, and two 'wild' tribesmen.

This historical European example serves to stress the similarities that occur when culture-contact involves the struggle for land. Throughout this book the same process will be found, of extermination, deportation and assimilation of natives who were considered uncivilized because they were different from their conquerors, and whose misfortune it was to occupy lands that they coveted. In each case local cultures were devalued and in many cases completely wiped out. In Scotland the Highland tribal system of government was utterly banished. Customs such as trial marriage were forbidden, the Gaelic language was suppressed and even the native costume was banned. Throughout the Highlands everyone was forcibly converted to the state Protestant religion. Clansmen were even deprived of whisky for a time, along with their firearms and any cultural items which could have interfered with their assimilation to an English, and hence 'civilized', way of life. The cleverest move of all, perhaps, was the sending away of Highland children to attend English schools. In due course the Highlanders were declared incapable of rapidly assimilating the new agricultural methods and their lands were then brought up to a 'civilized' standard by tenants imported from the Lowlands.

The North American Indian

In North America the policies and techniques of James I and Cromwell were applied with little variation: the populations were satisfactorily removed from fertile land through warfare, the deliberate spread of disease, the transfer of large populations to reserves and the psychological breaking of their spirit. The original Indian population was vast, that of Mexico alone being estimated at above thirty millions. Nowadays the number of Indians and Eskimos between the Rio Grande and the Arctic is just over ten million. By 1850 the Red Indian population had fallen to two hundred and fifty thousand.

The Indians fell victim to the white man because they occupied fertile lands eminently suitable to white settlement. First the river valleys went, then fertile grasslands, then forested lands, finally marginal lands, leaving the Indians with arid reserves which no respectable pioneer or

frontiersman wanted. Between 1887 (when the Indian Lands Act was passed to safeguard the Indian) and 1934, out of their allotment of one hundred and thirty-eight million acres, all but fifty-six million acres had been taken over by the whites. And when the Bureau of Indian Affairs examined these remaining lands, they concluded that fourteen million acres were 'critically eroded', seventeen million were 'severely eroded' and twenty-five million were 'slightly eroded'.

Like the Celts, the Indians resisted white encroachments on their land; in 1622, three hundred and fifty whites were killed – a terrible testimony to the failure of the New England Puritans to deal rightly with the Indians. After this the story is one of continuous cruelty, murder and enslavement; to enumerate the events that took place would be tedious in a book of this kind – since atrocities must be taken as the rule. For reasons of space, too, a summary must suffice.

In 1763 when the British army came to the aid of the settlers, the officers debated whether the Indians should

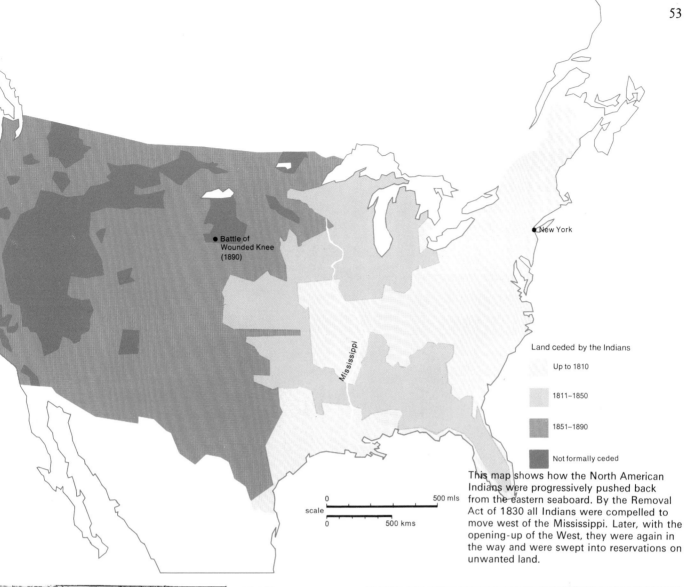

Battle of
Wounded Knee
(1890)

New York

Mississippi

Land ceded by the Indians

Up to 1810

1811–1850

1851–1890

Not formally ceded

scale

0   500 mls

0   500 kms

This map shows how the North American
Indians were progressively pushed back
from the eastern seaboard. By the Removal
Act of 1830 all Indians were compelled to
move west of the Mississippi. Later, with the
opening-up of the West, they were again in
the way and were swept into reservations on
unwanted land.

left Indians paddle out to welcome the
first landing in the New World of Columbus
in 1492; whereupon, he records in his
journal, 'I took some of them by force, to the
intent that they should give me information
of what there was in those parts'. **above**
A buffalo hunt, 1845. The buffalo provided
the Plains Indians with food, clothing and
shelter.

be hunted down with dogs or deliberately infested with infectious diseases. In those days especially, the methods used depended on the means at hand. Since there were no dogs available, the army distributed handkerchiefs and blankets from smallpox hospitals. Even Benjamin Franklin is quoted as saying that rum should be regarded as an agent of Providence 'to extirpate these savages in order to make room for the cultivators of the earth'.

Towards the Trail of Tears

After independence the United States government continued English traditions. The Removal Act of 1830 gave the president the right to exterminate all Indians who managed to survive east of the Mississippi river, as part of a plan to remove all Indians to new lands west of the Mississippi. The Cherokee Indians were among the saddest victims of this policy. In 1790 their chiefs and those of some other tribes had made a conscious decision to adopt the ways of their white conquerors, rather than be wiped out. The Cherokee, together with the Choctaw,

above Indian prisoners at Fort Bowie.
below Dakota Indians line up for rations at Fort Peck, 1908. The buffalo was almost completely destroyed by white hunters and the demoralized Indians came to depend for their survival on government handouts. When more Indian land was needed, rations were suspended until the Indians signed the land away.

above A Navaho child sits in the centre of a magical sand-painting. Once a simple, nomadic group, the Navaho later took to settled farming but then were starved out of their lands by the white man and removed to a reservation. There, however, aided by newly found mineral wealth, they have largely adapted to the white world around them.

the Creek, the Chicasaw and the Seminole became known as the 'Five Civilized Tribes'. In the Cherokee homelands, in the mountains where Georgia, Tennessee and North Carolina meet, farms, mills, schools, churches and even libraries were established. One chief, Sequoyah, perfected a method of writing in which English letters stood for Cherokee syllables, and by 1828 they were publishing their own newspapers. They had a constitution, with an executive, a two-chamber legislature, a supreme court and a code of laws. Then came the Removal Act and the Cherokees were on the wrong side of the line. Instead of being complimented for having made good, they were daily harassed by the government, subjected to atrocities by their white neighbours and bribed by federal agents to agree to their removal. Finally a minority of the twenty thousand Cherokee people gave in and were marched off; the rest clung to their farms and schools and churches. Then General Winfield Scott set about the systematic destruction of the remainder. Soldiers attacked isolated farms and marched families at bayonet point to their reserves. Their lands were taken over by whites. Some managed to escape into gorges and thick forests to become the nucleus of those living in the Great Smoky Mountains today, but most were killed or rounded up.

There followed a thousand-mile march, known by the Cherokees as the 'Trail of Tears', perhaps one of the most notable death marches of history. At least four thousand died *en route*. Families were separated when they arrived at their destination; the new lands were hardly suitable to Cherokee methods of farming, and different game needed different hunting techniques. They also encountered the hostility of the Plains Indians who had been forced to give up some of their lands to the eastern Indians; three thousand US troops were needed to protect the newcomers.

Despair in the West

That, briefly, is the story of the east. But no sooner were these tribes moved into the Plains than the resources of the West were discovered and settlers and miners were on the move again. Once again the Indian was in the way, a human obstacle to white expansion described by a Kansas newspaper as 'a set of miserable, dirty, lousy, blanketed, thieving, lying, sneaking, murdering, graceless, faithless, gut-eating skunks as the Lord ever permitted to infect the earth, and whose immediate and final extermination all men, except Indian agents and traders, should pray for'. At first the land-grabbers tried to restrict the Indians to useless land, but their efforts soon turned into a war of extermination. In the Plains the whites attacked the Indians' staple beast, the bison, on which they depended for food, housing, clothing and much more besides; the bison was totally destroyed. After the 1870s, when an élite Seventh Cavalry, organized specifically for killing Plains Indians and led by Lieutenant-Colonel Custer, had been annihilated at Little Big Horn by a combined force of Sioux and Cheyenne, troops began to pursue the Indians mercilessly from waterhole to waterhole, slaughtering men, women and children, and burning their encampments and their belongings. Their chiefs became miserable fugitives, survivors were herded into reservations where alcohol, disease and starvation reduced their numbers. The glorious Plains culture was at an end; the typical Indian brave in full regalia, trailing his war bonnet, astride a horse he rode bareback, today sweeps down on wagon trains only in glorious celluloid technicolour. The few survivors lingered on in despair, resorting to native messiahs who foretold the return of dead Indians and the magical disappearance of the whites. The United States government, alarmed at this spiritual insurrection, sent cavalry to suppress the 'Ghost Dance', as it was called. The famous chief Sitting Bull was arrested and accidentally killed; and some three hundred Sioux, mostly women and children, waiting to surrender in South Dakota, were massacred by trigger-happy troops at a place called Wounded Knee. This finally broke the spirit of the Indian nation.

America Starts a New Romance

In North America the Indians lost their land, and they also lost their culture. Orders were sent out from Washington in the same vein as those sent by King James I to Scotland. All male Indians had to have their hair cut short, even though to many of them long hair had a supernatural meaning. Children were shipped to boarding schools far from their homes. Their customs were ridiculed by their teachers. But then in 1932 came a reversal of policy: the government began to encourage the Indians to practise their old ways and their religion and speak their languages. Unfortunately for most tribes it was too late; but some had managed to survive with their cultures more or less intact. The Shawnee, for example, have held on to the remnants of their culture until today, maintaining their identity in the face of a white majority by developing strong anti-assimilation attitudes. The Navaho are famous for the success they have attained in a modern, western world.

Unlike hundreds of other Amerindian societies which are extinct today, the Navaho flourish on their reserve; with a population of about one hundred thousand they outnumber any other group of Indians. Their reservation, in Arizona and New Mexico, is also more prosperous than any other. They have mineral wealth and are now aggressively pursuing ways to make their agriculture more efficient, besides introducing a number of small industries. The tribal council has installed a computer to help it keep track of the tribe's monthly income of one million dollars, much of which comes from oil and mineral leases.

The Navaho are an interesting case: it has been suggested that they survived because they were a 'borrowing' people: they borrowed from the Pueblo Indians, the Spaniards and the Mexicans, and now they are borrowing from the white Americans. Yet they were once an exceedingly simple nomadic group; arriving among the Pueblos they turned to farming and absorbed their social and religious ideas as well as their rites and ceremonies. But when the white Americans arrived the Navaho were starved out of their lands; they signed treaties and finally surrendered, making a long trek into captivity at Fort Sumner, three hundred miles away, where they were placed in a reservation. But then, instead of declining, their spirit of enterprise led to further adaptations – tractors replacing horses and wagons, and factory-made utensils and tools replacing the old artefacts. The Navaho managed to turn the corner.

On the other hand, most Indians who refused to accept Americanization, who denied that the white man's world was the only place to live, remained hopelessly in their

left The frozen body of Big Foot, three
days dead in the snow after the massacre of
his band at Wounded Knee (1890), when
the Indians' resistance was finally broken.
below Today's Navaho is a strange blend
of Indian and western materialist, but his
lot is fortunate compared to the grossly
substandard lives led by most other Indians.

58

below A *churinga,* or totem symbol, that belonged to a member of the now extinct Arunta aborigine people of Central Australia. *Churingas* were sacred objects made of stone or wood and were believed to represent the spirit or essence of a tribe; in this case the totem symbol was a frog.

above Aborigine boys perform the dance of the brolga bird. Complex ceremonies were held to encourage the totem species to increase. This strengthened a tribe's sense of identity.

reservations, apathetic, unwilling to compete and desperately yet fruitlessly attached to their old ways and their old religions. Of those who went to the cities to find a new life, very few have successfully crossed the cultural divide and learned the acquisitive skills of the white man. And among the failures, alcohol and despair have taken a massive toll.

The American Indian today is, ironically, a hero; it is the pioneer white who is the villain. This can be seen in the attitudes of the new Western films and in the romantic interest that white Americans show in their aboriginal populations. Nevertheless romantic attitudes on the part of the dominant race do not make for rehabilitation. Today the average family income of an Indian family is only thirty dollars a week. The average life expectancy for males is forty-three; and the infant mortality rate is twice that of the Indians' white neighbours. And of the Indian infants who survive more than a quarter will die in their first year from a *preventable* disease. Despite the occasional success story the Indian's lot remains dangerously sub-standard in the language of white America and tragically unfulfilled in his own terms.

The Australian Aborigine

Land provided more than mere physical sustenance for the semi-nomadic Australian hunters. It was the focus of their social and spiritual life. Fortunately we know a lot more about the Australian aborigines than we do about the Tasmanians or even the American Indians, both of whom had lost their traditional cultures before scientific interest in primitive society developed in the late nineteenth century.

As far as land is concerned, we now know – contrary to what was supposed in the early nineteenth century – that the Australian aborigine was intimately attached to specific regions; he hunted only on his own territory, and rarely trespassed. Tribal ancestors had travelled those lands in the 'Dream Time' or mythical past, and established sacred places in them; and members of each group or horde were bound together by the common belief that spirits existed in that territory until they were incarnated, and that after death the spirits would return to the same territory. Thus when the whites robbed the aborigines of their land they not only parted them from physical resources to which they were accustomed, but they also wrecked their spiritual past and present – and their hopes for the future.

Australia is a strange land, a home still for quaint and exotic creatures that have elsewhere vanished and given

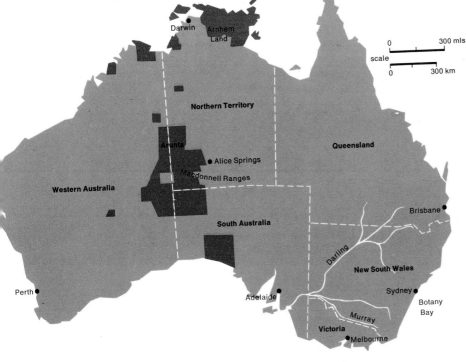

left Some 300,000 aborigines inhabited Australia's 2,967,909 square miles before the white man came; mostly they lived in the coastal areas but they were soon forced inland to more desolate parts when white settlements were established – at first in Sydney (1788) and around Melbourne. Today the aborigines are mainly restricted to the reserves indicated.

above Aborigine males sing sacred songs at a 'snake' corroboree or dance in honour of the tribal ancestors; this part of the ritual is followed by blood-letting and body decoration. left Their bodies painted, a group sits waiting for the dance to begin.

far left Aborigine crocodile hunters pass the time before nightfall — when the hunt begins — by drawing animal figures in the sand. left An aborigine corroboree ground at Yuendumu, Northern Territory.

place to other forms; like the platypus, which lays eggs yet suckles its young. The landscape is characterized by plants which are survivals of ancient floral elements that were once widely distributed, but have been crowded into extinction elsewhere by the spread of newer types. Where the platypus was seen as a 'missing link' between reptile and mammal, and the kangaroo as a modern representative of early mammalian forms, it was not difficult for early amateur scientists to attribute the same kind of odd position to the country's human inhabitants. The Australian aborigine for a long time suffered the ignominy of being thought a 'missing link', at least in the popular fancy, when in fact he is quite like most Caucasians, with his wavy rather than kinky hair, his hairy face and body, heavy brow-ridges and the depression at the root of his nose. The ancestors of the aborigine probably came over a land bridge from New Guinea which was connected by a chain of islands with Asia. This idea is reinforced by the aborigines' physical features, which ally them with small groups now surviving in out-of-the-way places in Ceylon, Malaya, Indonesia and New Guinea.

The only primitive quality about the aborigines was their means of making a livelihood. They were Stone Age hunters who roamed their territories naked, apart for a pubic apron for the women and a small pubic tassel of fur and string for the men. Their only other clothing were belts of human hair, nose-bones and head and neck bands; the hair was pulled out of the men's foreheads to give them an unnatural, balding look. Originally three hundred thousand Australian aborigines lived in the vast continent, the greatest concentration being in the coastal areas, but within a few years of the settlement of Sydney and the areas around Melbourne they were restricted to more desolate areas. There they lived dispersed, ranging widely to take advantage of variations in the seeding times of wild grasses and the migration of game.

The Arunta, now reduced almost to the point of extinction, are the most widely known aborigine group. This is because they received a thorough scientific investigation before their decline set in. In 1900 they numbered about two thousand: the men hunted with boomerangs and spears and the women scoured the land for seeds and bulb-roots, edible fungus, birds, eggs, snakes and the pupae of moths (witchety grubs), caterpillars, beetles, flies, honey, ants and any reptiles or burrowing rodents they could capture. The aborigines had struck an extremely fine balance with their environment and were wonderfully observant of changes in nature. The appearance of one object, a star, a bird, a flower, became, through their minute knowledge of their physical world, a sign that rain was coming or that certain fish were rising or that a certain animal would be plentiful. Yellow flowers of the wattle were a sign that the magpie geese would be flying along their annual routes, over the giant paper-bark trees from swamp to swamp to eat the lily tubers. So the men built platforms in branches of selected trees, and as they waited they mimicked the honk-honk of geese which then circled the trees and alighted. As they did so they were knocked to the ground with well-aimed throwing sticks and then were quickly dispatched by men waiting at the foot of the trees.

As we have said, the aborigines' close association with nature also implied a close association with the 'Dream Time', and his complex cosmology depended very much on his relationship with the horde territory which supported him. The cosmology or religion of the aborigines explained to them such phenomena as the seasons and the workings of nature; it explained the origin of their ancestors, in fact their entire culture. Their art, particularly the rock engravings, illustrated their beliefs in the Dream Time, when their ancestors made human beings from plants, animals and natural features. These then became the totems of modern groups.

A World of Totems

Totemism was perhaps the most important element in the Australian man-nature relationship. All members of a horde considered themselves descendants of a particular kind of plant or animal, and this was their totem. All the various totems had resting places in the land of the local group – which was also the home of the ancestral human beings of the group. When a woman who had married into a particular group became pregnant, it was believed that

below A scene from the early years of colonial rule showing aborigines being dragged along and beaten by white convicts.

her impregnation was caused by a spirit from the local totem, which had entered her body. The father therefore was not deemed to be the physical procreator of the child, only the social father, and the child was forever tied to that area of land because of the presence of the vital totem spirit. These are all important details to remember when we discuss the alienation of aboriginal land and the natives' removal to reserves. What the white settlers and administrators failed to recognize was that it was not simply a matter of moving a tribe of aborigines to another territory and telling them to get on with it. It was a removal in the most complete sense of the word, in which the living were abruptly severed from their culture.

The totemic centre of a community was the storehouse where the totem symbols (*churinga*) or fetishes were kept. In these objects resided the spirits of the whole group, including those of the ancestors; they were mostly flat, oval pieces of wood or stone carved with symbolic designs. Some had a hole near the end and could be attached to a string and whirled in the air to make the weird noise of the bull-roarer. This was used to keep the uninitiated, the women and children, away from the secret rites. The objects were vital and sacred symbols of the aborigines' ancestors. Their myths formed a meaningful symbolic code which was acted out in ceremonies; these ensured the well-being of the tribe by keeping them in touch with the creative Dream Time. The *churinga* or fetishes were concrete symbols of the Dream Time, and life and strength were conveyed through them.

Totemic ceremonies of increase were held at the time of the year when a particular species produced fruit or seed or gave birth to its young. They were complex rituals, mostly held in secret, and were believed to help increase the totem species; in this they were not unlike Christian harvest festival services. To begin with, part of the species was eaten by a specialist or priest before the initiated members of the tribe, while other elders each took a small part which was ritually consumed. This part of the rite parallels the Christian communion service. Finally there was a general feast, in which those not allowed to witness the secret ceremony also joined.

The secrets of these rites and the myths of the Dream Time were guarded by the tribal elders and handed over to younger generations at initiation rites. These rites involved ceremonial combats, feasting, dancing, body operations and ordeals. Initiation rites were vital to the well-being of the tribe since it was their main method of passing on their culture; they were also an important focus of aboriginal religion and helped to foster community spirit.

The aborigines lived at one with nature. Totemism, their religion, was a view of nature, life, the universe and man which coloured and influenced all aboriginal culture, inspiring their ritual and linking them to the past. To be able to pursue his life as a hunter the aborigine relied on nature taking its regular course; by performing various rites he made sure that rain and fine weather came, and drought and disaster were avoided. Totemism provided a link between everyday social life and the secret life of myth and ritual.

March of the Settlers

The English settlers – those who came to farm and graze – had no conception of the life and religion of the country's first inhabitants. As far as they were concerned Australia provided limitless land which was there for the taking; it was too bad if the 'blackfellow' was in the way. Cattle-herding and farming spread along the coast and then

left An aborigine hunter with his catch.
below A woman cooks a kangaroo,
holding it over the fire as best she can.

inland. The wheat, beef, wool and hides produced there soon became important factors in world trade. With the gold rushes of the 1850s the frontiers were pushed further and further back and the aborigines were separated from their land, their totemic spirits and their ancestors.

In the first stages the coastal aborigines, who lived in a fertile environment, suffered shock after shock. They fell back steadily before the white man, refusing to conform, losing their freedom of movement over their own country for social, food-gathering and ceremonial purposes. Diseases and violent death wrought their usual havoc and of the fifteen hundred aborigines in Sydney in 1788 only a few hundred remained in 1830; ten years after that the last remnants had disappeared, apart from a few 'tame' beggars.

In time the aborigines inhabiting the more arid central areas also suffered: in their case the suffering was caused by the expansion of cattle and sheep ranches. The 'glorious' period – as the white man saw it – of Australian expansion into the Outback offered no romance for the unfortunate aborigines; their waterholes were taken over, the totem species hunted out, their wives kidnapped, their children sent to mission schools and their manpower used as labour. The real tragedy arose from the fact that the aborigines then had nowhere else to go; tied as they were to their tribal territories by the strongest spiritual bonds, they were forced into accepting a new role in a white man's world.

Loss of Sacred Knowledge

This role meant relinquishing almost the whole of their traditional culture. With the disturbances and breakdowns brought about by the alienation of their lands the natives' skills deteriorated and their knowledge declined. Their secret life was mocked by settlers; missionaries were intolerant of their customs, instructing the young people to disobey their elders. Ancient traditions, such as initiation, were attacked; missionaries would obtain the sacred *churinga* totem fetishes from the old men under a promise of secrecy, and mock them in front of their pupils. Under the stress and strain of this new situation, in which the forces of law and order in the tribe were upset, the old men refused to pass on their knowledge to young men who had been seduced to white men's ways, and their sacred knowledge vanished altogether. Tribes lost the myths which ensured their well-being, and consequently fell out of touch with the Dream Time.

The three hundred thousand Australian aborigines of former times are today reduced to a quarter of their original numbers. Only a few hundred or so spend their time in the

left Aborigine shacks built from flattened kerosene cans in a reserve by the Macquarie River. below Daisy Bates, an eccentric who spent her life with a group of aborigines in order to ease their demise. She was wrongly convinced in the beginning that aborigine women ate any unwanted children.

traditional semi-nomadic way. Most are attached to stations and missions where they receive education, medical care, food, housing and employment. Many hang around towns and settlements, receiving odd jobs, begging from tourists and generally depending on the white man's bounty. The conditions in the aborigine slums of Central Australian towns are notorious; many live in rough lean-tos of old iron and tin, open to the sky, and rely on sacking or old clothes as protection from the wind and the rain. They have suffered a colour bar: special seats in cinemas are reserved for them and they are banned from some shops because local people say they are 'dirty' or 'smelly'. Some aborigines live at sheep and cattle stations on the uttermost fringes of civilization, while others are in camps for displaced persons or on mission stations. Alongside them, belonging to neither the white nor the black world, are twenty thousand half-castes who are unrecognized by their own white fathers and further regarded as socially unacceptable by colour-conscious white Australians as a whole.

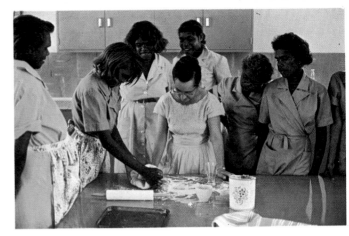

Today most aborigines are attached to stations and missions, where they receive basic care and employment. **left** A cookery class. **below left** A religious service at a Roman Catholic mission. **below right** An earlier picture (1949) taken before the shapeless, all-covering dress swept through the land.

Death in the Face of Progress

Until recently the Australian administration and the missions always 'looked after' the aborigine. This meant, however, that he was protected in idleness rather than encouraged to adapt to a new world – as he needed to do to survive. Mission stations were the cheapest way by which the government could ensure a minimal service to aborigines in areas where they would otherwise not have survived. There they were given rations and set to work carving curios ('witch-doctors' carved 'magic sticks'); they also received a Christian education. Unfortunately they were not taught to adapt to new ways in any practical, modern sense, and as a result hung around the mission stations, to the despair of their guides, taking to gambling, begging, drinking and – among the women – prostitution.

The semi-official attitude to the fate of the aborigines was that, like their Tasmanian cousins, they were doomed to succumb to progress. Many missionaries adopted the same attitudes as their colleagues in Brazil: the native would eventually die out and all that they could do was to 'smooth his dying pillow' and wait until he was taken into the bosom of God. In 1864 the Bishop of Adelaide pronounced that :'I would rather they died as Christians than drag out a miserable existence as heathens. I believe that the race will disappear either way. . . .' These beliefs (or perhaps it was wishful thinking?) were repeated by influential Australians right up to the mid-twentieth century. The popularly held opinion was that aborigines were biologically inferior and hence congenitally unsuited to civilization; the vicious corollary was that they deserved no better fate than a painless extinction. One woman, Daisy Bates, whose autobiography is widely read in Australia, continued this philosophy well up to our own times by spending much of her life among a group of Australian aborigines in order to ease their end. Among her original misconceptions was her strange and groundless conviction that Australian aboriginal women went on having children only in order to eat them.

For many years there was indeed some foundation for thinking that the Australians would follow the fate of the Tasmanians. Until as late as the Second World War they barely held their own: they succumbed to epidemics, and there was a continuous story of sterility, abortion, declining birth rate and very high infant mortality. Despondency and psychological decline due to the destruction of their culture and the failure of white Australians to put anything profoundly religious in its place was perhaps a major factor in their decline. This kind of despondency led to tribes like

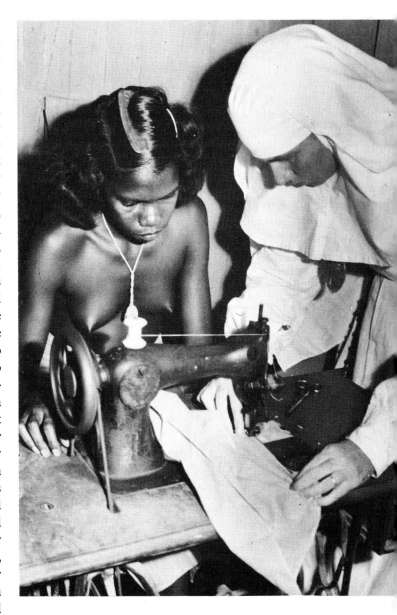

those of the Murray River destroying their half-caste children and even the majority of their full-blood babies. It is tragically illustrated in a dirge wailed to a traditional aboriginal air by the remnants of one tribe:

Where are my friends, my clanspeople?
Where are the Puntindjeri now?
I am looking for my friends, where are they?
I am lonely.
Where are my friends? Who is going to answer me?
They are all gone. Who is to answer?
I am lonely.
They are all dead my clanspeople.
Who is going to answer me?
I am sorrowful and lonely.

Revival of Black/White Hopes

But within the last generation, the aboriginal population has begun to make a come-back. Not only have numbers increased, the attitude of the government has also changed.

The policy now is that they are no longer to be protected and regarded as incapable of learning white Australian ways. After two centuries of exploitation, decimation and neglect the Australian government has begun to spend money on its wards and to listen to advice from experts. They are now to be assisted to achieve the full status of citizens within the mainstream of Australian society; in this they will receive incentive, and material help. At the same time white Australians are to be taught tolerance, understanding and a willingness to assimilate the 'black-fellows'. Government policy, at least, now declares that natives are free to become involved in white communities if they wish. They have already been given better educational and health facilities and their employment conditions have been improved. The federal franchise has been extended and they now receive equal social service benefits.

Is it too late? Like the United States government in the 1930s the Australian administrator wants the aborigine to continue to observe and practise his own customs, even to revive his ceremonial life in a modified form in order that

left Women and children shelter under a tree, displaying the kind of despondency that brought the aborigine race to the edge of extinction a generation ago. **below** Aborigines at a social gathering. The man in the suit, seen with some of the old men of his tribe, is a trained government teaching assistant. Today opportunities for the aborigines of Australia are much improved and their numbers have begun to increase again. Even so, they continue to be denied certain basic rights. In 1971 the Australian courts ruled that the aborigine had no legal title to any land in Australia, thus putting his homeland at the mercy of mining and other interests. White Australia seems determined to preserve the old colonial differentials between the haves and the have-nots.

he should re-acquire a sense of cultural belonging. Although aborigines will become Australian citizens, nevertheless it is realized that they are not white and that they should not be made to turn their backs on their own history and culture. They are therefore being encouraged to keep their own language, and to develop their own art and music and play a fuller part in Australian life – as aborigines.

These are fine words and the Australian aborigine has waited a long time to hear them. At Sydney University the Arunta language is being taught to white enthusiasts; the tribe itself is extinct. Australian artists, writers and composers are turning to the remnants of aboriginal culture for inspiration; but the aborigines themselves are hardly interested in this romantic revival. Although the future is optimistic and all is peace and quiet, the past is still present, as it is among the Indians of the United States and the Celts of Ulster. Black Power is even rearing its head among the black aborigines, who now find themselves living in a country dedicated to an immigration policy that excludes outsiders who are coloured like themselves. This is done in the cause of a 'White Australia'. The aborigines' resentment, hostility and sense of injustice may lead to a lack of co-operation with the well-intentioned anthropologists and administrators who are belatedly easing them into the modern world.

THE GREAT TAKEOVER

A society or a culture can disappear from the face of the earth in one of two ways: either its members are exterminated through disease and murder – which is what happened in Tasmania; or the society and its culture disappear but its original members and their descendants survive as part of a wider, much changed society.

The islanders of Hawaii belong in the latter category. In the early part of the nineteenth century they merged their Stone Age culture with that of a more powerful race. Today Hawaiian culture has nothing in common with the grand and elegant civilization described by Captain Cook when he discovered the islands in 1778. Descendants of kings and high priests, taro farmers and other clearly defined groups in the strict Hawaiian class system have been swamped by a tidal wave of Americanization. It began with the visits of whalers and traders in the 1800s, and continued with the determined activities of Protestant missionaries and pineapple and sugar-cane planters. This process entered a new phase in this century with the setting up of a high-powered tourist industry and a luxurious military establishment.

The proud Polynesians of Hawaii seem to have been the most supine of peoples in the face of European and American infiltration. Unlike the Tasmanians, the Hawaiians have made only isolated attempts to resist the imposition of western religion, morals, material culture and the usurpation of ninety per cent of their land. In this chapter we shall try to establish whether the complete physical and cultural assimilation of Hawaiian society to an international civilization has had positive results – in that the Hawaiians have avoided the epidemics, degeneracy and despair which have inflicted other, simpler societies when they were taken over; or whether they would have done better to eat every sailor, missionary and land-grabber who stepped ashore at Honolulu.

Hawaiians have never been conservative: for them new things have always been better than old things. This attitude, and their belief that foreigners who are superior in technology must also be superior in everything else, have been retained until this day in an uncritical admiration of all things Yankee or European. Cook was the first to

previous page Soft-eyed girls, glossier though less naked than they used to be, are a staple attraction of this archetypal Polynesian paradise, now a State of the USA. Today's Hawaiians take pride in being 100 per cent American, and their tourist industry works hard to satisfy the dreams of visitors in search of the old-time culture.
right Early Hawaiians, from the days of first contact with the white man, hunting sandpipers by beating at them with branches.
below An offering is made before Captain Cook, who discovered the islands in 1778. After his death in a skirmish the following year, Cook's body was divided up, burnt and the bones scraped as befitted a chief or god.

note it: 'They could not help expressing their surprise by a mixture of joy and concern . . . and on all occasions they appeared deeply impressed with a consciousness of their own inferiority.'

The respect given to Cook, for example, the first white man to visit the island, amounted to worship. It was adoration at first sight. The very instant he stepped ashore he so dazzled the populace that they fell flat on their faces. Cook was taken for Lono, one of their gods, who had left Hawaii one day promising to return in a floating island covered with trees. Cook curiously suited the legend of Lono, a god of rain and crops, who presided over the *makahiki* season when taxes and tribute were paid to the chiefs: Cook himself arrived during this season on each of his two visits to the islands. Unwittingly he further encouraged the people's belief by setting up an astronomical observatory in one of the local temple sites. Cook was thereupon submitted to god-like rather than guest-like treatment, enduring interminable rituals and listening for hours to what to him must have been mumbo-jumbo. In

the end, however, he was killed in a skirmish with the natives; nevertheless, his body was divided up, burnt and the bones scraped as befitted a chief or god.

A Hawaiian Golden Age?

The Hawaiian Islands, or Sandwich Islands as Cook named them, stretch in a chain some four hundred miles long across the Tropic of Cancer. Seven islands are inhabited, and since 1959 the group has been a state of the USA. The ancestors of today's Polynesian inhabitants had migrated from South-East Asia as long ago as the second century AD, settling in Samoa, Tonga, the Society Islands and the Marquesas before arriving in their seventy-foot double-hulled canoes in Hawaii in the seventh or eighth century. They came with their families, bringing livestock and provisions in the form of dried food, and the seeds and tubers of hibiscus, yam, taro, gourds, *ti* (for making barkcloth), sugar-cane, bananas and sweet potatoes. Their migration was as least as adventurous as the well-equipped journeys of farmers, soldiers and convicts who set out from

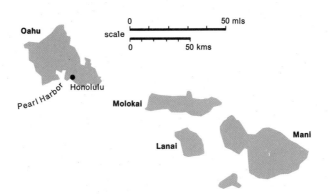

Kanai

Niihau

Oahu

Pearl Harbor Honolulu

Molokai

Lanai

Mani

scale
0   50 mls
0   50 kms

The Hawaiian Islands are situated in the North Pacific on approximately the same latitude as Mexico City; the distance from Honolulu, the capital, to San Francisco is 2,100 nautical miles. The islands cover a combined area of 6,424 square miles; seven are inhabited and their population in 1970 was 748,600.

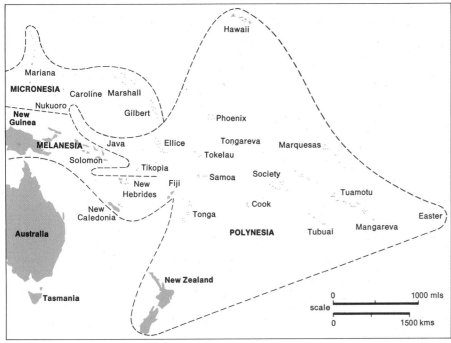

left This ethnic area map shows the triangular shape of Polynesia, with Hawaii at the apex of the triangle. The ancestors of today's Polynesian inhabitants migrated from South-east Asia to Samoa, Tonga, the Society Islands and the Marquesas as early as the second century AD; Hawaii was settled later, in the seventh or eighth century.

below The High Chief Boki, a governor of Oahu in the early nineteenth century, with his wife Liliha, who wears a lei or circlet made of human hair to denote her rank. The early Hawaiians lived under a rigid class system that included separate layers of aristocrats, priests, commoners, and an outcaste slave population that performed the menial tasks.

England for Australia more than a thousand years later.

During their first thousand years the Hawaiians remained undisturbed and developed their own brand of Pacific culture. In technical achievement it was a Stone Age culture – though the term is inadequate for describing such complex systems as Polynesian economic and social organization. Wealthy chiefs ruled over a sharply defined class system. Commoners worked the farms and fished, while an outcaste slave population – having no caste or rank – did more menial jobs. There was a closed group of priests who were also master craftsmen and used their skill to celebrate the gods, whom they represented by images of wood, feathers and stone. This group was even more dreaded than the chiefs, and its members were said to be able to pray a person to death.

The social system was supported by taboos and *mana*. *Mana* is a powerful kind of supernatural, impersonal force, which according to Hawaiian belief the nobles possessed. The greatest chief – belonging to an unblemished lineage kept pure by incestuous marriages between brother and sister, and descended from the gods – had the greatest *mana*. And while the chiefs had *mana* the lower classes had the taboo (Hawaiian *kapu*) of defilement, and were debarred from contacting their superiors. Taboos thus protected the aristocrats from the contamination of commoners and nearly all activities were affected by this weird system. Severe penalties, such as strangling or clubbing, were

inflicted for offences involving royalty. The system of taboos was the keystone of Hawaiian culture. Temples, idols, sacred places, priests and fathers of families were protected by them. They gave supernatural sanction both to the caste system and to the inequality of the sexes: women were denied certain foods, such as pork, and could not eat with men or enter places where men worshipped. Chiefs enjoyed lives of luxury and ease, usually evident in their excessive corpulence, 'their flesh lying in deep folds about them, their walk a majestic stagger'. They lived in large, beautifully decorated houses and wore the marvellous bark-cloth, as fine as gauze, decorated and dyed in shades of pink, yellow and pale blue. They wore helmets with waving plumes and fine feather capes made of 'the most beautiful red and yellow feathers, so closely fixed that the surface might be compared to the thickest and richest velvet' (Cook). One of these capes, made with feathers of eighty thousand rare birds, now extinct through the introduction of a European disease, was presented to King George IV.

But the wonderful islands of Hawaii were wonderful only for the rich and aristocratic: commoners endured hard work, grim sanctions and rigid discipline. The chiefs were elegant, but they were also demanding and overbearing. A lieutenant in Cook's party describes one of them, a magnificently regal youth who visited their ship in a double canoe, paying no regard to smaller canoes which happened to be in his way – he simply rammed them with their occupants inside as he passed. He was surrounded by retainers who protected him from commoners by holding hands in a ring around him. And on board ship, every time the chief went below decks, all the Hawaiians on the ship dived into the sea in order to avoid breaking the serious taboo against having their heads higher than that of a noble.

Invasion by Whaler, Trader and Missionary

Once Cook had broken Hawaii's thousand-year isolation, there began an influx of foreigners. This resulted in the unchecked retreat of the native culture before western morals, economics and religion. From 1840 onwards no one could doubt that the fate of the exotic Hawaiian was to be absorbed by the North American Republic. Within a generation Hawaiian culture was virtually extinct.

The whalers and traders were the first main group of *haole* (white men) to come, and this initial period of contact was a disastrous one. Diseases such as measles and whooping cough decimated the population; firearms were intro-

above A Hawaiian lady dressed to go riding; her costume – which usually looked more imposing once the wearer was astride a horse – was designed to avoid the discomforts of riding side-saddle over uneven ground. Aristocratic Hawaiians were protected by a system of taboos from the contaminating influence of commoners. Offences against the system carried severe penalties, such as clubbing or strangling.
left King Kamehameha I (1758–1816), who launched a campaign of conquest throughout the islands following the death of Captain Cook in 1779; although he was held at bay for some years by the ruler of Oahu, Kamehameha finally invaded that island in 1790 with a fleet of 1,000 war canoes and quickly overran it; the remnants of the defending army were forced over the edge of a precipice. During Kamehameha's reign trade with the outside world was rapidly expanded and this caused the downfall of Hawaii's ancient religious and social systems; islanders were corrupted by the introduction of alcohol and firearms, and sex became commercialized to suit the appetites of visiting traders; old beliefs that threatened to impede this so-called progress were swept aside.

duced and the rulers, particularly King Kamehameha I (1758–1816), came to exploit their subjects still more; alcohol became a serious threat to a population unused to any kind of fermented drink; children learnt to smoke as soon as they could walk; and with the arrival of each ship fresh waves of venereal disease swept the islands. Europeans seemed to 'hang up their consciences on Cape Horn'; and the free and generous attitude to sex of Hawaiian women soon became corrupted by commercialism as well as by disease.

The most remarkable incident in the drastic Europeanization of Hawaii was the abolition of the system of taboos. King Kamehameha I came to the throne after the death of Cook in 1779 and extended his wealth and power by selling sandalwood to traders, who distributed it in Asia and Europe as a base for incense and for use in cabinet-making. The sale of sandalwood became a royal monopoly and this brought about a swift decline in the island's balanced social and economic system. For a few years Hawaiian aristocrats lived well on the profits from sandalwood cut by commoners at their own expense. Fourteen sailing ships, bales of the best silks, liqueurs, tableware and clothes from Europe were among the purchases that the Hawaiian chiefs paid for in sandalwood.

Meanwhile, however, the old world of taboos was fast crumbling before the activities of Europeans who ignored them. After the death of the king the whole framework of traditions, based on *mana* and *kapu*, was allowed to collapse. It was Queen Kaahumami, the king's favourite wife, who determined the taboos should finally go. At a great public feast she and other women ate forbidden foods, and the new king joined them and ate with them. After a moment of silent shock the crowd gave a roar of delight, realizing that the taboos were at an end. 'The gods are a lie,' they shouted. All at once, as if the keystone of an arch had been removed, the infrastructure of an entire ancient religion and social system collapsed and was abandoned.

A few months later the first missionaries arrived, convinced that the removal of the taboos was the work of the Christian God. The missionaries were Calvinists and they had heard of the wickedness going on in the Hawaiian islands; so they determined to travel to the South Seas and bring the islanders to the 'Mansion of Eternal Blessedness'. Their expectations of wickedness were immediately fulfilled as they watched the Hawaiians swimming out to their boat to welcome them. The ladies looking overboard suddenly felt faint and giddy. 'Some of our number,' wrote the Rev.

Hiram Bingham, 'turned away from the spectacle of the half-naked Polynesians with gushing tears. Others with firmer nerve continued their gaze, but were ready ·to exclaim: "Can these be human beings!? How dark and comfortless their state of mind and heart!! How imminent the danger to the mortal soul, shrouded in this deep pagan gloom!! Can such things be civilized!? Can we throw ourselves on these rude shores and take up our abode, for life, among such people for the purpose of training them for Heaven?" '

Fortunately, for the Rev. Bingham at least, these 'children of nature' were eminently civilizable. The first lesson – that nakedness was sinful – was soon learned. The women were made to cover their provocative bodies in a shapeless garment, soon converted with a flounce and a frill into the famous Hawaiian *muumu*; and the men wore trousers and shirts. Wealthy Hawaiians easily adapted to the change. A German traveller, Otto von Kotzbue, wrote: 'My guests had all dressed themselves in their best attire. I scarcely recognized Kareimoku, who shone in the dress of

an English pilot, with polished boots and a cocked hat; but all his things were too tight, that he could scarcely move a limb, and the noon-day's heat threatened to stifle him in his costume. . . . The Americans certainly buy up in their cities all the clothes which are out of fashion and sell them here to great advantage.' And one princess, instead of elaborate bark-cloth robes, was wound into seventy-two yards of cashmere, so that her arms stuck out horizontally and she had a hundred-foot train behind her as she walked to church. If this seems an extreme example it is included because the Hawaiians were accustomed to extremes. In contrast the common peoples' clothes consisted of vermin-ridden rags which they never removed. Disease was rife.

Within eight years the missionaries had huge congregations and after sixty years seventy thousand Hawaiians had been baptized. New taboos replaced the old ones: against fornication, tattooing, stealing, against working on Sunday and making orange rum. Along with Christianity the natives were made familiar with book-learning, cake-making, sewing and singing. Frame houses, teetotalism

top left Hawaiian washerwomen in the period following the massed advent of the Protestant missionaries, from whom the islanders learned that nakedness was sinful.
left Street vendors in Honolulu with their baskets of leis; already the search for tourist favours had begun. **above** A group centred round Queen Liliuokalani, the last of the native monarchs, who reigned briefly in

the 1890s before a republic was established in 1894; in 1898 the USA annexed the islands, which then became official US territory in 1900.

78

Oriental workers in a pineapple cannery. By 1900 white settlers owned four times as much land as other nationalities; to work their sugar-cane and pineapple plantations migrant labour was brought in mainly from China, Japan and the Philippines; by 1950 Hawaiians, now mostly of mixed blood, made up less than a fifth of the population.

and bonnets helped turn wicked Honolulu into a New England country town. Economic domination soon followed. By 1900 *haole* owned four times as much land as all the other nationalities. This had happened because the chiefs had gradually, though not in any systematic fashion, given up their lands to European sugar-cane and pineapple planters and cattle ranchers. The old hereditary ruling class of nobles was replaced by a ruling caste of white bankers, traders, planters and missionaries.

The Hawaiian Melting-pot

Since the initial white invasions, the major impact on Hawaiian life has come from two other no less important invasions: those of the oriental labourers introduced to work the plantations, and of the millions of tourists who have poured into the islands during this century.

When the Hawaiians' irrigated farms and unoccupied land had been converted to sugar-cane and pineapple plantations, the local inhabitants shunned the monotonous work and returned to their coconut groves and fishing, or drifted to the towns. The *haole* were then forced to go to the ends of the earth to get labourers. Chinese coolies were brought from the Canton delta, but in time they gave up plantation work to open shops and a fresh supply was introduced from Japan in 1868. After the 1890s consignments of Portuguese, Filipinos and Puerto Ricans followed, and by the beginning of the twentieth century the Hawaiians were outnumbered in their own houses. In 1950 the figures for the different races in Hawaii were as follows:

Hawaiian	86,000
Caucasian (white)	115,000
Chinese	32,000
Filipino	61,000
Japanese	185,000
Korean	7,000
Negro	3,000
Puerto Rican	10,000
Other	2,000
	501,000

This meant that Hawaiians had become less than twenty per cent of the population, and of this quota eighty-five per cent were of mixed blood. Given the great variety of exotic peoples now in the island the racial result will inevitably be a complete assimilation of the Hawaiians; and the Japanese, already strong, will come to predominate. Europeans in Hawaii, particularly Americans, continually sing the praises of what they consider to be a perfect racial mix; but they forget that the mix was accidentally achieved.

left and below A surfer prepares a board, while another is shown on the brink of action. Surfing originated in Hawaii, where it was first performed as a kind of ritual, later banned by missionaries who suspected it of being a licentious activity; later still it was taken up on a worldwide scale and transformed into a massive leisure industry.

All the whites ever did was to shuttle in one race after another and let them get on with it. The *haole* are still the most influential race and when the melting pot has fully melted the cultural traditions will be almost entirely white and American.

Americanization has already happened. Language in Hawaii is ninety-nine per cent English. Chinese rituals are in English and only a few scholars and one or two aged Hawaiians speak any Polynesian. Even Buddhism is, in Hawaii, an Americanized kind of Christianity with Dharma and Buddha instead of the Holy Spirit and Jesus. Old Hawaiian culture only exists for the tourists. Hawaiians are devoted instead to American fashions, hairstyles and

fads, and are keen followers of US football games, which are relayed from the mainland by satellite. Hawaii is now simply another example of Americanization, whereby the culture of heterogeneous peoples has been watered down to fit into a general pattern of American life. Despite the Japanese teahouses, the Singapore banks, the Ka Palapala beauty contest, Aloha Week, the Cherry Blossom Festival Queen and Japanese *bon* dancing, Hawaii is one hundred per cent American and proud of it.

A Virgin Island

Could the loss of an entire ancient culture have been avoided? One of the islands, Niihau, has tried. This island is owned by the Robinson family, originally sheep-farmers from New Zealand, who bought the island from the Hawaiian king in 1864. Alarmed at the Americanization and demoralization of mainland Hawaiians they turned their island into a private refuge for the local inhabitants, allowing no visitors, no dogs, no films, no police, no tobacco and no alcohol. Residents of the island and the owners travel to the mainland by sampan. In order to keep their blood pure, their morals unaffected by white vices and their temperaments docile, these few hundred brown people have been virtually isolated from the world. Church services and school classes are conducted in the Hawaiian language, and if an inhabitant leaves the island he is only allowed back if his family wants him.

But it is hard to believe that the old Hawaiian culture is in fact being preserved, since the islanders had already been Christianized and taught to wear clothes before the experiment began. Its effects cannot of course be observed since no visitors are allowed, but its continued existence seems to underline the eccentricity and possible dangers of rejecting any kind of social, economic and political adaptation. In essence it represents a reduction to absurdity of the idea of isolating the native for his own good and keeping him in a kind of human zoo, permanently conditioned by traditional values.

The Visitor Industry

Today Hawaii is flourishing as a result of wars and tourism. From Pearl Harbor supply-ships steam silently out with bombs for Vietnam and return with cargoes of wounded men and newly filled coffins. Hawaii depends on the military, deriving a huge income from US defence sources which have to pay for looking after a military population of a hundred thousand people, as well as – until recently – almost two hundred thousand soldiers a year on R and R

Four views of the land below Diamond Head, the site of an extinct volcano on the island of Oahu, as it changed from a sleepy bay in 1857, **above,** to a place for white visitors to bathe and fish; as its popularity grew, the name of Waikiki Beach travelled round the world and the sea gradually turned dark with holidaymakers. From a small village Honolulu became a major city and a polished international resort dominated by luxurious hotels and the Ala Wai Yacht Harbor. Inside the crater of Diamond Head (a final futuristic touch) is an installation of the Federal Aviation Agency which is used to monitor aircraft operating in the central Pacific Ocean.

(rest and recuperation) – together with a corresponding number of 'loved ones' from home.

Still more important from the point of view of the local population are the tourists: by 1978 Hawaii expects three million tourists a year, four times its population; the islands seem at times to be sinking into the sea under the weight of their tourists.

Known officially as the 'Visitor Industry', tourism has brought about what the Public Relations men call a 'renaissance of Hawaiian culture' – though in reality this merely means that the few Hawaiians who remain, and any inhabitant who can be passed off as Hawaiian, are encouraged to cling to their old ways for tourist appeal. In the same way as General Franco enthuses over regional Spanish dances and costumes for tourist purposes but demands total conformity in the religious and political areas of culture, the Hawaiian is expected to live up to the tourist stereotype and at the same time conform to Yankee sentiments and values. Descendants of kings and slaves, indistinguishable in crew-cuts and gaudy shirts, turn the

In time the Hawaiians converted more and more of their old customs into cabaret acts. **above** A float in the Aloha Week parade, well stocked with bikini girls. **below** Wiggle time for American ladies attending a hula class; the hula was originally a sacred dance that was later simplified and pepped up for the tourist market.

islands into one huge romantic and sentimental Disneyland, where the attractions are the remnants of a derelict Stone Age culture.

To the American tourist the Hawaiian stereotype is that of a quaint, promiscuous, friendly people, who live in an unspoilt world, have cute babies and are wonderful dancers. At home, however, the Hawaiian throws off his *leis* (the traditional circlets of flowers) and his permanently welcoming *aloha* grin, drinks coca-cola instead of kava, eats rice instead of *poi* (taro pudding) and dances to the strident beat of rock music rather than the romantic whine of the ukelele.

The tourists find what they want. They eat Hawaiian feasts cooked in steam from stone ovens in the gardens of their hotels. They undergo ceremonial kava-drinking. They watch a genuine Hawaiian sitting in a thatched hut eating *poi* and swarm around anybody on the beach who is mending a fishing net or scraping down a boat. They learn surfing from beach boys who parade Waikiki Beach, and have their tired American bodies massaged in the old Hawaiian way. After dinner someone announces that 'ladies and gentlemen will be entertained by Joe Kahoa with his native flame dance'. And in front of the aircraft which is to take them away, they sing to the ukelele and the garlanded wives wiggle their newly learned hula dances. Tough businessmen sing a song of farewell:

When we say goodbye,
Don't be afraid to cry

their cheeks temporarily awash with tears.

For the American Hawaii is a dreamland of golden people, living in a perfect state of contentment, away from the rush and strain of his own world. It is an artificial paradise, on which the white man projects his repressed desires – to do the things he would do if he were not tied down by the tedium of American social and economic morality.

For the Hawaiian, however, the Visitor Industry may prove disastrous. Sentiment of this kind is dangerous to a people's dignity, and the Hawaiian is fast becoming a tourist object. The natives are considered simple, shiftless and mindless even by university professors and local dignitaries. 'The islands are like wombs,' wrote one. 'The Pacific Ocean is the amniotic fluid in which all our students are immersed. They are so secure they do not have to think.' The government, the missionaries and the Visitor Industry are careful to look after the Hawaiians: they attend richly endowed schools, belong to exclusive clubs

and are given protected jobs. That, at least, is the surface picture. In fact they are being pushed to the wall, touted, tormented and patronized by the system which supports them.

Hawaiian Culture Today

The Hawaiians have borne the brunt of a cultural and population invasion with admirable docility. Yet they have lost their culture and they are about to be bred out by their guests. Societies equally hierarchical and taboo-ridden have managed to salvage a good deal of their cultures – the Ashanti and Yoruba in Africa are good examples. The Maori of New Zealand, themselves Polynesians, have restored themselves to a position of pride and hope in a society which is predominately European. The Hawaiians, on the other hand, have lost their culture, probably because the impact of trader, missionary, politician and business magnate was so swift and so concentrated.

But what of the arts, Hawaiian music, legends? Has the tourist industry not led to a conscious cultivation of things

Flowers with everything: lei sellers woo opulent tourists with their garlands. Such is the power of the 'Visitor Industry' (as the tourist trade is known in Hawaii) that a reversion to old ways would now be unthinkable – as well as almost impossible.

above A Sunday ceremony at the
International Market Place, near Waikiki,
where Hawaiians put back the clock and
roast a pig, island-style, for the entertainment
of visitors. **right** Time off in paradise for
US sailors and their wives, who try on
exotic Hawaiian costume. Today Hawaii is
home for a vast military establishment and
a playground for some 200,000 soldiers
annually on R and R (rest and recuperation).
Who weeps for the old Hawaii ? Probably
very few even recognize the passing of this
ancient Polynesian culture, perhaps because
the impact of trader, missionary, politician
and business magnate has been so swift and
so concentrated.

Hawaiian, such as singing, bark-cloth making and sculpture? These are reasonable questions; but sporadic manifestations for the benefit of a tourist industry have, unfortunately, nothing to do with the revival of a culture.

The Hawaiian culture which a tourist experiences is entirely artificial. The genealogical songs, the poetical chants, the elaborate old musical instruments such as the gourd *hula* drum are all gone. Myths and stories are remembered only by scholars. The famous Hawaiian featherwork and sculpture is found only in museums or made by imported American experts. The entire picture is a sad one, a loss for the Hawaiian and for the world. Hawaiian traditional legends and chants were wonderfully original but they have not been drawn on for a single classical literary work. Even the celebrated inter-racial democracy of the twentieth century has had no impact on the arts. Hawaiian huts, oriental temple styles and western buildings have produced no recognizable synthesis. Western music has obliterated old Hawaiian music without leading to a blended style. Even the ukelele is an import from Europe and the Hawaiian popular music which we associate with the South Seas is purely Euro-American – a bastard product of Portuguese and Latin American rhythms and Protestant hymns. All this can be said equally about the famous *hula*. Again, there is little connection between the strange swaying taught to foreign matrons and performed by girls in hotel gardens, and the authentic Polynesian *hula* – which was a sacred performance and would certainly bore the great mass of tourists. So, to placate the majority, a ritual dance has become musical-comedy wriggling.

Surfing, or wave-sliding, is probably the only genuine Hawaiian contribution to world culture. Nevertheless it too has become quite a different thing from the complex institution it was in the past, when it had religious, sexual and gambling connotations. Naturally frowned on by the missionaries, it almost perished during the nineteenth century and only recovered when Americans took up the long, heavy boards and popularized it as a sport throughout the world.

The Future

The Hawaiian today is a blend of several races and several cultures. Of course we must deplore the loss of almost every element of a wonderful Polynesian culture, but perhaps it is right that Hawaiian blood should soon be merged with the rest of the population, contributing to its good looks and providing an injection of hedonism which

is badly needed. It is certainly a preferable alternative to their remaining a tiny minority of specially privileged 'natives', kept as pets for the benefit of tourists in islands they once owned. We can express regret that the first European settlers, particularly the missionaries, were too busy substituting their own myths to make any attempt to preserve the culture and oral traditions of the local inhabitants.

All the same, the Rev. Hiram Bingham would very likely spin in his grave if he knew about the new Hawaii. Waikiki Beach throbs again with music and half-naked abandon as alcohol-swilling, pagan New Englanders pour into Honolulu every year to re-live a little old-time Hawaiian culture. The outer islands shelter groups of gentle flower people and hippies who fly into Hawaii and set up communes in groves and sugar-cane fields. And in the port of Lahaina, beards, male earrings and tooth necklaces are appearing around the wharves for the first time since the sworn enemies of the missionaries, the whalers and sealers, disappeared a hundred years ago.

THE RIGHT
TO STAND APART

Extermination, genocide, extinction, murder, rape, race suicide; much of the evidence in this book has a sensational aspect. We have seen how whole worlds, cultures and societies have suffered at the hands of technologically superior peoples. In these circumstances culture contact seems always to mean culture conflict – the survival of the strongest or largest number. This, happily, is not the only possibility; there are other examples of peoples who have determined to survive the depredations and colonization of invaders; or who have managed to survive over the centuries in contact with dominant neighbours.

African societies have long histories of adaptation to a continually changing situation. They have met and coped with western industrialization, Christianity and Islam, as well as conquest by indigenous empires. As a result their cultures are neither static nor isolated but include elements in their religion, art and social organization that come from every possible source. Traditional huts are embellished with European chairs and china; women have 'discarded' their nakedness for striking national costumes made from foreign cloths. European beer is drunk alongside palm wine. A local chief takes off his fine robes and plumed hat to put on a European suit when he drives to town to sell his coffee. He adds, for good measure, the name of the European god to those of his ancestors when he prays at the local shrine. His children are christened and sent to school.

But many Africans oppose the assumption that the world of Western Europe and America is the best of all possible worlds. They refuse to do what the foreigner (whether district officer or missionary) considers 'good for them'. That is why the African continent still shelters countless languages and diverse peoples who not only survive in diversity but flourish. For centuries communities of farmers, hunters and gatherers, fishermen and nomadic pastoralists have lived side by side, adapting to each other's needs and accepting each other's idiosyncrasies. One of the best examples of a very simple culture which has survived despite intimate contact with peoples who are technologically or numerically superior are the cattle-herding Fulani of West Africa.

88

previous page A Fulani cowherd brings his cattle to water. For centuries the Pastoral Fulani have wandered freely over the savannah lands of West and Central Africa, grazing their animals and moving on, giving their allegiance to none. **below** A slender, bronze-coloured Fulani girl tends a herd near Tahoua, Niger.

right Six million Fulani, a nomadic race probably of Berber origin, live in a broad band of savannah some 3,000 miles wide which stretches from Senegal as far as Sudan. Although the Fulani live at peace with the local landowners, their code forbids them to mix with other cultures except to trade with them – selling milk to buy corn, etc.

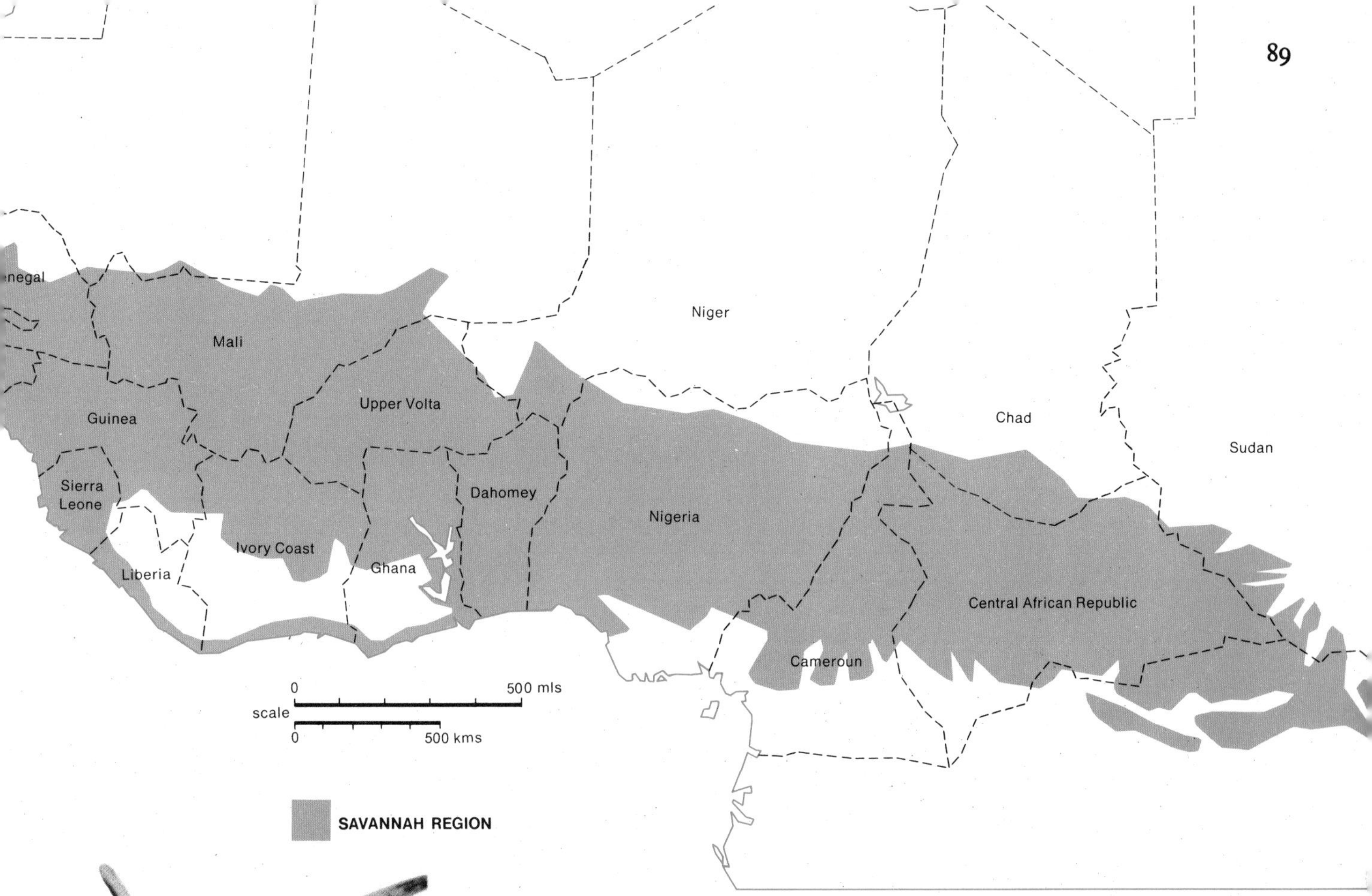

Mali

Niger

Guinea

Upper Volta

Chad

Sudan

Sierra
Leone

Dahomey

Ivory Coast

Nigeria

Ghana

Liberia

Central African Republic

Cameroun

```
        0                    500 mls
scale  |___|___|___|___|___|
        0                    500 kms
```

SAVANNAH REGION

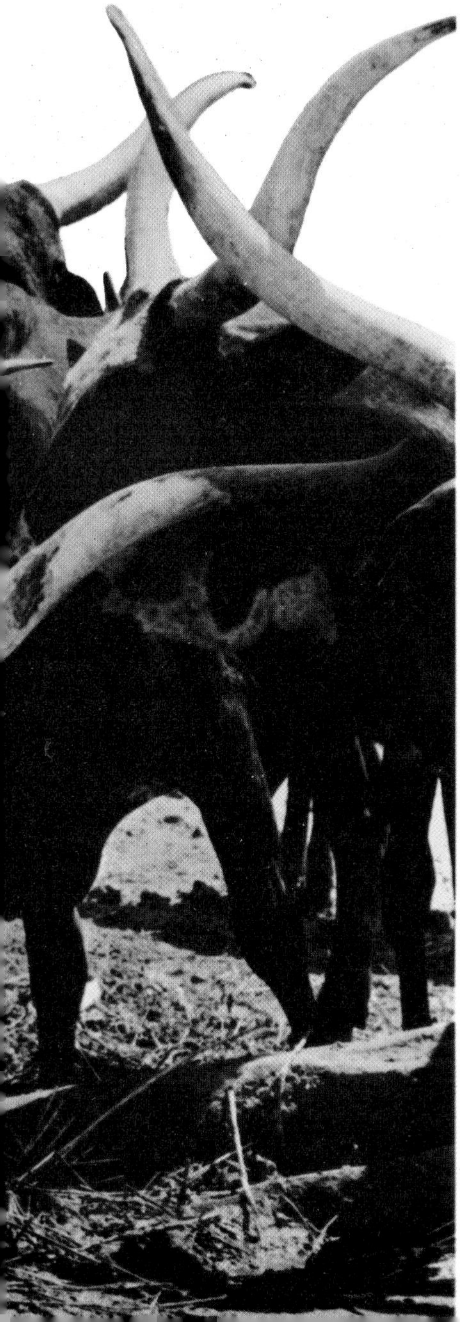

The Pastoral Fulani

Right across West Africa from the Atlantic to the equatorial forests of Central Africa live the Pastoral Fulani, a people who have exercised the imagination of novelists, historians and anthropologists alike. They are slim, bronze-coloured, elegant cattle people who have grazed their animals for centuries across the lands of pagan farmers, Moslem kings and European colonialists, giving their allegiance to none as they moved from territory to territory in search of peaceful pastures. They have always been the 'mysterious' people because of their striking looks, their pride in their simple way of life and their aloofness from the worlds both of Negro farmers and of westerners. Why do they look so different from other Africans? And where did they come from? They have been confidently explained as a lost tribe of Israel, as Syrians, Gipsies, even a Hindu caste. In reality their origins are not so very romantic: they are probably of Berber (North African) stock and moved down the west coast of Senegal about a thousand years ago, where they acquired the language they now speak. Since that time they have wandered across the whole of the savannah regions of West Africa.

What concerns us here is how the Fulani have managed to expand from a small community of North African migrants into a vast population of six million people; and how, though scattered over such a wide area, they have retained their language and their unique racial and cultural traits, while intermingling with farming peoples of completely different languages, culture and race. We are at present dealing solely with the Pastoral Fulani. But it is as well to mention also the groups of Town Fulani who have hived off from the Pastoral peoples to form fixed village settlements. There are, too, Fulani chiefs and emirs who as a result of religious wars conquered pagan and Islamic

above From childhood Fulani boys are
prepared for a lifetime of cattle-herding.
Before they receive their first calf, the young
boys learn by watching their elders.

above and left Without the cow the culture of the Pastoral Fulani would collapse, and within a generation or so they would merge into the settled world of their farming neighbours. Here the usable innards of a slaughtered cow are sorted, and strips dried over a slow fire.

chiefdoms, and whose descendants – also known as the Fulani – rule over large Negro populations right across the area travelled by the Pastoral peoples.

Copper-skinned Cattle Farmers

Six million people spread over a three-thousand mile stretch of bush and grassland sounds like a vast world, but within it independent Fulani communities are very small. Their very presence is not at all obvious to the traveller as he drives for miles past the farms and villages of the Islamic Hausa, the circular huts of the pagans and the flat-roofed market towns with their busy stalls and mosques. The Fulani keep away from other people, but across the fields you may catch sight of a tall, copper-skinned boy playing his flute as he watches a milling herd of cattle or another like him leaning against one of the cows for support, caressing its lyre-shaped horns and chanting to it in a soft voice. Even their camps blend in with the bush; their household equipment is meagre and their temporary shelters are made from branches torn from a nearby tree. Within hours they may strike camp and disappear like the wind which blows through the bush; and when they have gone, all that remains is a few stripped branches and a patch of bare earth.

This temporary, camouflaged homestead is the real world of the Fulani, the formal centre of life which shifts with them as they lead their cattle from the dangers of the tse-tse fly or to a distant water hole. When they arrive at their destination a patch of earth is cleared, a calf-rope is set up and the women erect their frame beds and store away their bundles of ceremonial clothes, jewellery and decorated calabashes. This 'patch of earth' is an important ritual space; within it the Fulani family and their cattle act out strictly patterned lives. There is a 'front', which must always face west. This is divided in two by the calf-rope, making strictly demarcated men's and women's sections; the rough bed-shelters are set up in a carefully observed north-south orientation. The physical structuring of this space – the calf-rope, the corral fire, the women's beds and the young men's mats – all serves to channel the day-to-day activities of the household. It also symbolizes relationships between different members of the household. The women's side of the calf-rope is reserved to them and their children, although their husbands visit them for sex. The other side is the sacred preserve of the men and the cattle, the women only entering it in the morning and evening to milk the cattle. Within the men's section there are areas reserved to the older men and the youths. Young

below Women pounding grain in a settled Fulani village. **below right** A woman and child riding on a pack-ox, near Ayorou, Niger. Once married, a Fulani woman devotes herself to providing children for her husband and to milking his cattle and selling the milk.

married men whose wives are still childless sleep with them on mats outside this circle. Women never eat with men – in fact they should not even see them eating. A man eats his food alone, with his back to the group, and the youngest is always last. The herd mills around the fire in the men's section at night and their formation, too, oddly reflects the formality of the Fulani family; the bull lies nearest the fire, the stronger cows next to him but a little apart, while the young bulls and the heifers remain on the edges and the calves are tethered to the rope which divides the Fulani homestead.

Growing up among the Fulani

Fulani boys learn their masculine roles early. From childhood a boy is immersed in the world of cattle, even his games are conceived with a life-time of cattle-herding in mind. Little boys dig tiny dry-season wells and model cows, calves, bulls and pack oxen in mud. After circumcision a boy moves out of the women's half, crossing the calf-rope to sleep on the men's side. He receives his first leather wrap and his first calf, and begins to imitate the older men in their handling of the cattle, caressing them, singing to them, removing their ticks. As he grows up he becomes betrothed and watches his own section of the herd grow.

His wife learns to milk and make butter from an early age. She learns to rub the teats of the cow to encourage the milk, blowing up the vagina of a really stubborn one. She may hold the hide of a calf which has died while her mother milks the cow, squatting behind. She will go to market with the other women, balancing a small calabash on her head, walking up to ten or fifteen miles to sell a pint or two of milk in exchange for some millet corn. These groups of Fulani women are a memorable sight as they go across the open fields, their calabashes on their heads, straight-backed, with their seductive and undulating walk. Their long hair is plaited in elaborate braids, their faces are made up and jewellery cascades from their hair, their ears and their throats. But, like their menfolk, they are unapproachable; once their milk is sold they start off on the long walk home, indifferent to the approaches of the boisterous Hausa traders and other market sellers.

Once she is married a woman's business is to provide children for her husband and to apply herself to her role of milkmaid and milkseller. The birth of a child proves her fertility and not till then does she move into the women's world and acquire her own bedstead. Husband-and-wife relations are formal and business-like; the woman takes a secondary role. The word for 'woman' in Fulani comes from the root 'to follow', and follow she does. The social and moral code of the Fulani demands from her a life-long attitude of restraint and obedience. Women at the age of sixteen give up their sexually free life to marry and work and produce children. The poetry and demonstrative affection of lovers are things that the Fulani prefer to keep out of the business of marriage.

As her daughters grow up and marry, they take with them a portion of a woman's precious horde of decorative calabashes. When her last daughter marries and her calabashes are finished the woman's role in this milk-extracting, child-producing corporation comes to an end. When a man hands over his last cow to his last son his productive life also comes to an end. Their status as old men and women is not high and often they cease to live together, and instead move into rough shelters in the homesteads of different children. When they die they will be buried beneath the spot where they slept; they are already socially dead, and exist, as it were, over their own graves.

A man's life is spent pasturing his cattle, seeing to their needs, curing their illnesses and drawing water for them from deep wells every morning and evening. Cows are beloved members of the family, known by name and treated with an affection amounting to devotion. If a man loses his cattle through disease, his world comes to an end; in such cases a Fulani has been known to go mad, tearing off his clothes and wandering naked through the bush calling the names of the dead beasts. Looking after cattle is their only fully rewarding occupation and they never complain of the hardships it brings. In the wet season particularly, when the cattle are herded together in restricted pastures away from the tse-tse fly, they have to be watched night and day. Herds stampede at the sight of strange cattle moving in the bush, or through sheer excitement when they feel the pouring rain after months of drought. Hyenas abound and annoy them. For the men at those times there is the extra work that must be done of de-ticking, felling trees for fences and seeing to the seasonally increased amount of animal sickness.

94

right A market in Niamey, Niger. A Fulani woman may walk up to ten or fifteen miles to market with a calabash on her head (**below and opposite**) to sell a few pints of milk and buy some corn. Her decorative calabashes are handed down to her daughters as they grow up; when her calabashes are gone, a woman's useful life is over.

A Fulani composes poems to his cattle:

My cattle arise and go, they make the earth tremble,
They shake the trees, divert the streams,
Muddy the pools, and clear the thicket.
My cattle bellow, the antelopes flee.
My cattle bellow, it puts the buffaloes to flight.
My cattle bellow, it sets the baboons barking.
It turns the deer away, and brings good fortune near.

The rocky heights have baboons, I have cattle . . .
The mountains have springs, I have cattle . . .
The streams have fish, I have cattle . . .
The rivers have water, I have cattle. . . .

Festivals of Endurance

It is towards the end of this tiring wet season that larger groups come together for group discussions, naming and circumcision rites and the paying of taxes to their clan leader, who passes them on to the local administrator. This is also the time of dancing, dressing up and sexual escapades, when eleven months of hardship and the continual fight for survival are forgotten in a period of intense social life. The *gereol* dances are now held – wild competitive games between clans in which both boys and girls take part. There is a good deal of sexual licence, the boys chasing the girls who are their age-mates, catching them and making love, a group of age-mates often sharing a willing girl.

The most spectacular of the Fulani games is a sado-masochist test of endurance which youths undergo at this time. A boy of about sixteen chooses a challenger. Beautifully made up and wearing an ornamental kilt and other trappings, he prepares himself to be whipped by his challenger, watched by his age-mates, older youths and a complement of maidens.

He holds his arms above his head, and languidly fingers a necklace or gazes at his painted face in a mirror while his challenger deals him two vicious cuts across the ribs. As the girls and his age-mates watch, the youth receives the blows without wincing, without even moving a muscle or crying out, so seeming to mock his challenger's strength as

he preens himself in the mirror and ignores the blood which drips from his chest. Drugs are sometimes taken during these games and induce a passionate sense of excitement in the group. The test of endurance perfectly expresses the values of the Fulani pastoralist, his calm acceptance of hardship and pain.

Pride of the Nomad

This brief sketch of the Fulani way of life shows a world which has been maintained with few modifications over hundreds of years, surviving epidemics, wars, pressure from Islamic groups and colonization. The Fulani have not achieved their freedom through complete isolation, how-ever, nor through a completely self-subsistent economy. They live in a fairly inter-dependent relationship with those Negro farmers over whose land they roam. How is it that the Fulani have resisted all temptation to adopt the settled, less strenuous life of these farmers? How have they managed to survive with their simple cattle-economy in the face of external pressures? How have they maintained their Fulani culture and the Fulani appearance?

Perhaps the prime reason for their survival is that they occupy an environmental niche which has not been coveted by more powerful groups. Their expansion over the savannah lands of West Africa has caused little conflict since they are lands which are mostly ill-suited to agri-

above Ankle ornaments worn by Fulani girls. Before marriage the girls are allowed a sexually free life that flowers most intensely during the annual clan meetings. **right** Fulani youths made up for a dance.

culture. The mere fact that they are nomadic, that they can always 'get up and go' means that there is little time for miscegenation, or mixing with other cultures, where the young might learn the ways of the towns or be seduced by the pleasures of European consumer society. But this by itself is not enough to ensure continuity, and among the Fulani any temptation to settle down to a farming life is countered by intensive and continual propaganda to encourage a belief in the beauty and the satisfactions of their own way of life, which is inculcated in children from their earliest years. The Fulani are perfectly conscious of the fact that to remain Fulani in a motley and frequently hostile world needs constant application.

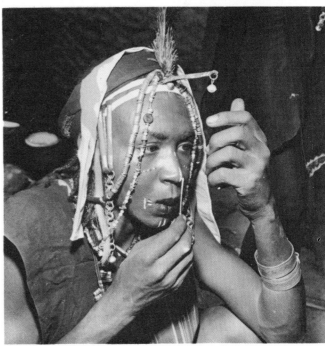

above Fulani youths preparing for the annual dances and the wild, competitive games that take place between clans on these occasions; both boys and girls take part and most games have a strong sexual element.

98

A man's herd of cattle, as the be-all and end-all of his life, confers on a Fulani all the social prestige he needs. Hence their reputation for being poor traders and bargainers, their lack of craftiness in business matters being part of their traditional system of values. They sell their cattle only when they have to, in order to pay taxes, though this is usually done when their beasts are in a scraggy condition and prices are low. They buy millet corn when prices are rising and salt during the scarce period when the salt caravans have not yet arrived across the desert. Ecological conditions determine their refusal to think about the economics of life, not their backwardness or single-mindedness. They have no desire for cultural novelty or consumer goods simply because these things would upset the *status quo* and disturb the delicate balance between the Fulani family, their cattle and the environment.

Their lack of enthusiasm for cultural change is deeply engrained. Few of them ever learn the language of their Negro hosts, for example; and in many places it is their own language that has been used as the common one. It is true that they have adopted Islamic prayers and routines, their years and days being divided up by Moslem rituals. Yet this is part of their practice of adapting as far as possible to the milieu in which they live, accommodating themselves to the demands of their environment rather than opposing them. As far as his general outlook is concerned, however, the Fulani is not a Moslem; in the

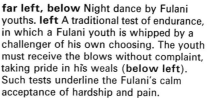

far left, below Night dance by Fulani youths. **left** A traditional test of endurance, in which a Fulani youth is whipped by a challenger of his own choosing. The youth must receive the blows without complaint, taking pride in hǐs weals (**below left**). Such tests underline the Fulani's calm acceptance of hardship and pain.

practical and mystical field of religion his place is still deep in the pagan world.

Fulani values are expressed in a code which every child learns, a traditional system of ethics which bolsters the Fulani way of life, stressing right conduct, assuring peace in the community, and the fertility of cows and their women. The qualities they value are modesty and reserve, fortitude in the face of adversity and a lasting devotion to the needs of their cattle.

The Marriage Code

A practical example of the Fulani code is the way they regulate marriage. The Fulani are divided into patrilineal clans, that is, clans in which descent is traced through men. Clans are subdivided into lineages. Usually in Africa marriage is forbidden within the lineage or clan, and is instead exogamous (or practised outside the clan); but among the Fulani the most highly valued marriage is endogamous – practised within the lineage, and preferably, for a man, with his father's brother's daughter. As is the custom among most Africans bridewealth is handed over by the groom and his relatives to the kin of the bride. Among the Fulani cattle are wealth and when there is a marriage some cattle are given to the bride's people. If a man marries a woman of the same lineage, the bride-cattle are kept in that lineage – as is the woman. This form of marriage helps to provide cohesion in the Fulani world, keeping their blood pure and their cattle together. The practice tends also to mark the Fulani off, not only from their Negro neighbours, but from other groups of Fulani. Like a particular herd of cattle a lineage may become noted for certain stereotyped characteristics – specially straight noses, long hair, tallness, the copper hue of their skins.

Endogamy – marriage within the group – expresses their desire to keep themselves to themselves; as a people they show a passion for exclusiveness which is one of their most striking features. The Fulani are very suspicious of all strangers and their reticence can make the friendliest advances come to nothing. Their confidence is gained with the greatest difficulty and is easily lost. The Fulani simply do not like other people: at the market the men and women keep to themselves, refusing to mix with other ethnic groups. Children are taught by adults that people who do not follow the Fulani code are savages, who live in the bush only waiting to do them down, to kill their cattle, make them pay taxes and convert them to another way of life. The Fulani way is, therefore, a narrow track through this bush with the Islamic townsmen on one side and the pagan farmers on the other. The pagans are likened to hyenas because they are shameless enough to go naked in public and even eat food in front of their wives and children. The idea of having sex with a pagan is compared in horror with the experience of eating the fruit of the bitter, black plum tree. The worst punishment for a Fulani who has committed a crime is to have his clothes removed and to be banished to the pagans' 'bush', like a wild man. Their dislike of strangers affects their relations with Europeans, the Hausa and also the other Fulani who have slipped away from the narrow path of nomadic pastoralism and have settled in villages; they refuse to allow their cattle to come into contact with a 'degenerate' Fulani, whom they accuse of bringing and spreading disease.

Building a Sense of Superiority

This antagonism to other races, coupled with the desire to retain a minimum of economic relations with other peoples for the exchange of necessities, helps the Fulani acquire a sense of moral and physical superiority. This is demonstrated by the inordinate pride they take in their own appearance. To a remarkable extent the Fulani code has enabled them to retain their paler (or redder) skin and finer Mediterranean-type features. That, of course, is the 'ideal' Fulani type; in most Fulani several hundred years of residence in West Africa have left some signs of Negro admixture.

Racial pride is consciously engendered. A young mother massages the cranium of her newborn child as if to model it into the desired shape – a kind of elongated sphere. She spends hours manipulating the nose of her baby son between her fingers as if she were trying to make it long and thin, vainly attempting to give it an elegant aristocratic line in sympathy with the forehead. From childhood the Fulani are taught to take a pride in their bodies, painting and decorating themselves, pulling their hair into intricate shapes. Girls are taught the graceful undulating walk which marks them off from Negro women, whose gait is more steady and purposeful-looking.

Survival of Simplicity

By such methods the Fulani world has managed to survive external pressures. They have paid tribute to kings, made obeisances to colonial rulers and missionaries and paid taxes to nation states. They have kept on terms with Moslem farmers and put up with the enforced vaccination of their cattle. Around them African peoples are adapting to the new values of the twentieth century, taking to Islam and Christianity with enthusiasm, altering their age-old economic patterns, enjoying consumer products introduced from the west.

The survival of the Fulani is at first sight remarkable. Yet they have been facing change and attack from many quarters for almost a thousand years, and most probably they will continue to wander 'uncontaminated' across the savannah lands unless these lands become ecologically valuable to more powerful groups. So far oil has not been discovered, nor is the growth of cash crops for export a profitable proposition in this area. Another factor is that the Fulani family or lineage – a man and his wives and his sons and their wives, with their herd of thirty or forty cattle – is not a very vulnerable group. The missionary and the administrator have not succeeded in regimenting or changing this simple social structure. It has proved sufficiently pliable and adaptable to change, unlike some Negro farming societies whose complex organization of clan structures, age grades and secret societies that cut across the community and ritual kings and priests crumbles before the march of colonialism and nationalism.

Of course, fresh dangers may arise. New diseases might wipe out their herds and in these days the Fulani may lack the wherewithal to start again. National governments, sponsored by world organizations, are encouraging all children to attend schools; and once Fulani children are taken away from their cattle and the homestead calf-rope, and taught the kind of western values which are everywhere taught in African schools, they will learn new ways. They will meet Negro children, they will enjoy football instead of their dances and whipping matches. Missionaries from the United Nations may come and tell them to love their neighbours and stop despising the pagans, on the assumption that all problems are solved if all men are equal and treat each other like brothers. Missionaries of our capitalist world will certainly try to teach Fulani children the pleasures of our consumer goods, encouraging them to increase their herds in order to sell them for cash. Already the requirements of twentieth-century Africa are making their mark: national jealousies are beginning to prevent the Fulani from wandering from territory to territory or from state to state in search of new pastures. Bureaucracies require individuals to be citizens of one state. If the Fulani learn modern techniques of herding, if they are told it is wrong to marry close cousins, in all kinds of ways the beginning of the end may be near.

Nevertheless the situation is a hopeful one. In many

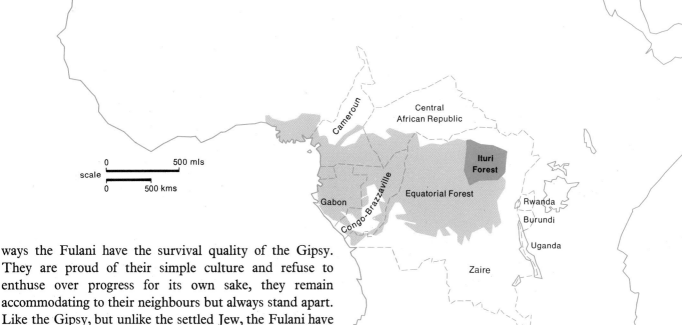

above The equatorial forest regions inhabited by Pygmy peoples reach across the boundaries of many modern states, including Congo-Brazzaville, Zaire, Central African Republic, Cameroun and Gabon; a few Pygmies are also located in Uganda and Rwanda. The chief concentration is in the Ituri Forest, where some 40,000 live.

ways the Fulani have the survival quality of the Gipsy. They are proud of their simple culture and refuse to enthuse over progress for its own sake, they remain accommodating to their neighbours but always stand apart. Like the Gipsy, but unlike the settled Jew, the Fulani have remained racially distinct – chiefly because they are always on the move. The main ingredients in the Fulani's survival are thus the cow and their nomadic way of life. Take away these and their culture would disintegrate, and within a generation or two they would merge into the world of their farming neighbours.

Upheaval and Change in Africa

The Fulani are not, of course, the only Africans who have maintained their own way of life amidst racially and culturally different peoples. The continent of Africa has hundreds of different languages, hundreds of different worlds, all of which flourish in their diversity, despite the seemingly overwhelming pressures of colonialism, neo-colonialism, labour migration, land expropriation, urbanization and insistent propaganda from missionaries and the Peace Corps and their like.

Change, conflict and new ideas have always given spice to life in Africa, often reactivating tribal values and a sense of cultural identity. We are far from the sensitively isolated worlds of the Tasmanians and the Tierra del Fuegians.

The Pygmies: People of the Rain Forest

The Pygmy people of the Congo rain-forest have preserved their unique culture and racial characteristics despite constant contact with farming neighbours who are both numerically and technologically superior. The Pygmies are nomadic, like the Fulani, and make their livelihood from hunting game and collecting wild fruit and roots. The forest is the Pygmies' home, a dark cathedral of gigantic trees, the ceiling a tracery of dripping foliage which forms a constant barrier against the sun. Negro farmers, living on the edges of this forest, find it a forbidding place and use their Pygmy 'slaves', as they regard them, to procure game and other forest goods for them. But the Pygmies are not strictly slaves – the two peoples lead economically interdependent lives, similar to those of the Fulani cattle herders and their Negro neighbours, except that the Pygmies exchange game for farm products and the Fulani milk for grain.

After many thousands of years in the forest the Pygmies have become physically as well as culturally adapted to their environment. Unlike the tall, black Negro, they are short, and have pale yellowish skins, downy body hair and

above A group of Ituri Pygmies constructing the roof of a hut in their forest camp. The Pygmies spend the major part of their year in the silent, mysterious heart of the forest, having little contact with their Negro neighbours.

right Two Pygmies examine a sample of honey before they decide how much to take from the nest. **below** This group is discussing the suitability of a site for building a new hunting camp. The Ituri Pygmies are a proud and independent people; despite pressure from farmers and mining interests, they have so far successfully preserved much of their culture.

head hair which grows in peppercorn tufts. Such is the extent of their bond to the forest that attempts by well-meaning administrators and missionaries to free them from it, or even from their client relationship with the Negroes, met with enormous difficulties. In the first place the inter-dependence between Pygmy and Negro (in what is called a symbiotic relationship) is mutually advantageous, each providing the other with essential services while main-taining their separate cultural identities. Both Negro and Pygmy have a healthy contempt for each other's way of life, each other's intelligence and each other's appearance. The Negroes pity the Pygmies for having to live in the forest while the Pygmies laugh at the Negroes' fear of the spirits and mock the clumsy farmer when he tries to move about in it.

So far only a few Pygmies have been persuaded to leave the forest and set up camp beside their Negro 'masters', where they have become tourist attractions, posing in clothes they would never wear in the forest, and selling weapons which they got from the Negroes. The forest Pygmies pour scorn on these degenerate 'monkeys' who ape the real Pygmies for the benefit of passing white men, in exactly the same way as the Pastoral Fulani bitterly attack their settled cousins. In the short space of one or two generations Pygmies who have moved to the edges of the forest acquire Negro physical characteristics, values and behavioural patterns. There seems, in fact, no hope of Pygmy groups surviving either physically or culturally outside the forest.

Resistance to Government Schemes

The Pygmies' home is being cut back every year. Once, two thousand years ago, the Pygmies had the whole equatorial forest to themselves. Then the migration of the Bantu Negro into this zone meant that the Pygmy was pushed further and further into pockets of the great forest. Now there are about 150,000 of them restricted to the forests of Central Africa, and even these are being threat-ened by mining interests and farmers. The situation almost exactly parallels the advance of European sheep-farmers into the lands of the Australian aborigines, which was discussed earlier. The only difference is that there is much more tolerance, much more give and take between the Pygmy and the Negro farmer. Nor has the Negro ever felt the need to 'convert' the hunters to his ways and his beliefs.

Of the total of 150,000 remaining Pygmies, some 40,000 live in the Ituri Forest in N.E. Zaire (former Congo-Kinshasa). In the Congo before independence, Belgian policy had always been content to leave these people as they were, mainly because they lived in an inaccessible and un-profitable part of their colonial domain. Recently however, changes have come about. Large clearings have been made outside the forest and government-built Pygmy settlements have been organized. The Pygmies at first reacted enthusi-astically to the free tools, the seed corn, schoolhouses and dispensaries. But the plan failed; the Pygmies went back to the forest, ate the seed and sold the tools to the Negroes. They took the view, 'Why should we work our farms when we can steal from the villagers, anyway?' The problem will not become serious until the Pygmy environment totally disappears. They have survived for thousands of years and are certainly not going to give in now. Their life is in the forest and they are standing out against any merging of cultures, forced or otherwise. The older men preach a strong resistance to all changes. 'We are the people of the forest and we have no need to fear it. We are only afraid of what is outside the forest.' They know, and so do the administrators, that Pygmies cannot survive in the open lands outside the forest. They soon become ill from diseases which they have not met before; they cannot even drink water which is completely harmless to sedentary Negro farmers and Europeans. In one model village for Pygmies twenty-nine died in a single day, primarily from exposure to the sun. It is the old, old story and any careless regi-mentation or too eager plans for reform may bring further, like disasters.

The intermixing of races as a means of solving con-temporary African problems is a recipe that would fail anywhere on the continent. Pygmies and Fulani have not survived by defying the presence of Negro farmers; the arrangements they live by are co-operative and more subtle. The conflict which results from cultural differences, a dash of xenophobia and racial pride are often necessary to reinforce a tribe's cultural identity. On the other hand we should not insist on preserving the *status quo* regardless, since adaptability to a changing environment is as much part of the African's make-up as it is of the European's. Even the simple lives of the Fulani and Pygmy have been enriched to a certain extent through contact with their neighbours.

Chapter 6

HOPES FOR SURVIVAL

The story of the disappearance of so many primitive worlds is at once sensational and pathetic. Telling the story is not by itself enough, and in this chapter I want to discuss some constructive ideas for helping the members of simple societies to adapt to the modern industrial world and also to present one or two cases of cultures which have successfully bridged the gap between 'savagery' and 'civilization'.

It is clear that the 'human zoo' solution – shutting peoples away the better to protect them – is not to be recommended. We must not romanticize primitives' way of life and decide on their behalf that they are enjoying the best of all possible worlds – as the good New Zealand family did for the Hawaiians of Niihau, who were then frozen at a convenient stage of their evolution. In many cases primitive life *is* 'nasty, brutish and short', and consequently it should be recognized that some peoples are keen to improve their lot by the advantages and magic of civilization. However, acculturation – the thorough adaptation of a people to an alien culture – and integration – the fusion of one culture with another – are both difficult processes which have not been given serious practical consideration until the present time.

Various organs of the United Nations, enlightened governments and colonial powers are contributing a good deal towards the emancipation, education and health of their minorities or subject peoples; but very little has been done towards helping their indigenous cultures to survive. To many communities out-and-out progress and total assimilation to the twentieth-century world of the west means extermination. That is why experiments like that of the Xingu Park are invaluable. Whatever means are adopted in helping people like the Australian aborigines and the Brazilian Indians, changes must be brought about slowly in order to minimize the shock that must accompany them. Today, fortunately, the fate of peoples is being decided more and more according to humanitarian rather than economic criteria: however, since this costs money and brings in no material rewards the difficulties are great.

The old misconception that primitive peoples are unable to change from the Stone Age to the Space Age because of

previous page A stilt-house dweller walks ashore in New Guinea. There, contact with white culture has proved a comparatively successful experience. This is partly because the peoples of New Guinea – fishermen, sailors, hunters and farmers alike – embraced the white man's arrival without fear.

their 'small brains' and their low intelligence has now been dispelled. An equally dangerous notion, however, supposes the answer lies in 'welfare', to guarantee at least a minimal standard of living; and that governments and missions are already doing enough. Unfortunately combinations of kindness, food and clothing, while they improve the situation, cannot close the socio-economic gap between 'native' peoples and their 'civilized' (better-off) neighbours. That is the kind of welfare that belongs rather in prisons, zoos, slums and old men's hostels. Natives not only have to be protected from land speculators, tourists and bigoted missionaries, from disease and sexual attack; they also have to be taught to *understand* the new culture which has spread across their lands. Without an intelligent appreciation of the new way of life they will never benefit from our schools, our medicines, our tractors and our gods. We have seen many examples of people who have not been able to adapt, and this is not because they are physically or intellectually incapable of joining up with our culture, but because either they have never begun to learn to appreciate it or they have not been given the time to come to a full appreciation of it.

Many peoples, among them the Australian aborigines and the Brazilian Indians, are not used to being curious, acquisitive and imitative. Unlike ourselves in the west (and also many peoples in Africa and New Guinea and other parts of the Third World) individuals are positively taught not to show curiosity. Among the Australians, for example, most members of a tribe grow up knowing that much of their culture is restricted to one or more groups and is not free for all. They do not pry into white men's ways. The Indian looks quietly at the ground instead of eagerly at the strange jeep or the missionary's wife's weird hair-do. This is because learning in these societies is directed towards a continuity with the past; imitation is therefore a matter of imitating the traditional, not the strange and new. Nor do these people understand our passion for acquiring property: food is collected to eat at once while other goods are manufactured for immediate exchange. Awareness of the benefits of owning land, of money and material goods has to be acquired through learning about them. As we shall see in the case of New Guinea, a tradition of acquisition and a greed for gain are great advantages in adapting to the modern capitalist world.

The problems of teaching western ways to such people are delicate and complex, and should obviously not be left to chance, to inexperienced governments or missionaries who have been programmed chiefly for other activities.

below A Maori get-together in New Zealand. Although the Maoris, a Polynesian people, were converted to European dress and customs some 150 years ago, they have retained their cultural independence through faith in their own traditions.

Administrators, United Nations experts and all those people interested in human relations should be made aware of the problems. It is not yet clear to what extent the cultures of primitive groups can be preserved, but much can be done to restrain industrial society's powers of annihilation over men and their civilizations.

One organization which has been established to work for this end is Survival International, formerly called the Primitive People's Fund, which came into existence during the summer of 1969 following widespread publicity given to Brazil's Indian Protection Service. Because of the interest aroused over the atrocities committed against the Brazilian Indian and the rather wild talk at the time of genocide, this London-based charity considered it appropriate that its first major project should be undertaken in Brazil. With the help of gifts from sympathizers, Survival International plans to make grants for specific action to help primitive peoples in urgent need in the Americas, Eastern Asia, Oceania, Australasia and Africa. As far as Brazil is concerned it has found that any speeding up of integration and indiscriminate contact would be disastrous. The problem is great since the Indians are scattered over huge forest areas and their circumstances are very varied. However, it is clear from the report prepared by the society that unless something is done immediately, few if any of the Indians who remain uncontacted, or have only been recently contacted, can be expected to survive the next ten years. Through research and publicity, Survival International is informing the public of the value to civilization of the culture of primitive peoples. The organization has plans to combat disease and to educate the people concerned to adapt to a changing world without losing their cultural identity. It is also preparing to fight to prevent the destruction of original environments, so that primitive peoples can continue their own lives securely if they so desire.

Almost all experts are agreed that a total assimilation of marginal peoples to the dominant culture is not immediately – if ever – desirable. Facts seem to show that except in special cases a complete mixing of cultures results in the inferior group suffering from mental and physical disharmony as well as a general feeling of social inferiority. The Hawaiian case seems to demonstrate this. The best policy would seem to be to encourage increased respect for local cultural traditions and to maintain and even increase the cultural status and numbers of minority groups in the Americas, Australasia and Africa.

In this way ethnic differences will be recognized, tolerated and valued. Such a policy of integration – as opposed to assimilation – would mean that equal opportunities would be available to all, the natives being free to become fully involved in the wider community while observing and practising their own customs. This seems the best goal in the modern world. The peoples affected could then decide for themselves if they wanted to submit to a complete biological, cultural, social, and economic assimilation – and at the same time to allow their culture to be lost through absorption.

The Maoris of New Zealand

A good example of integration without assimilation is the case of the New Zealand Maoris. Here a people has

above The heavily tattooed face of a Maori, recorded during Captain Cook's circumnavigation of New Zealand in 1769. The lines are carved into his face.

below A Maori war canoe. Ornately decorated vessels brought the Maoris to New Zealand from central Polynesia in the tenth and fourteenth centuries.

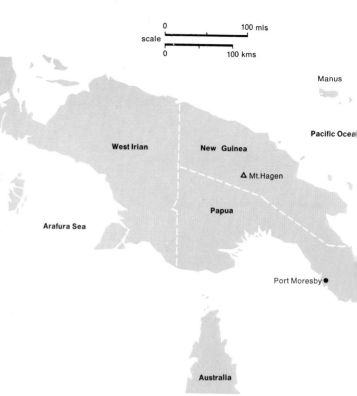

right New Guinea is the second largest island in the world (321,000 square miles). It lies approximately seventy miles north of Australia at the nearest point; the Australian trust territory of New Guinea also covers the islands of the Bismarck Archipelago, including Manus, and the north-west Solomon Islands. The population of the mainland is about 3,100,000.

retained its cultural independence and racial pride without turning its back on the white man's ways or his know-how.

The Maoris are a Polynesian people, like the Hawaiians. They are an exceptionally capable people, and when contact was first made with Europeans they already had a developed social structure, an artistic tradition and an economic system. Their history in many ways resembles that of the Hawaiians except that, unlike the latter, their culture still flourishes today and is recognizably Polynesian. The Maoris initially came into contact with Europeans during the first half of the eighteenth century, at a time when transactions between whalers, missionaries and traders remained spasmodic and uneventful. Later, particularly in the 1830s, the Maoris were impressed by the white man's techniques and enthusiastically adopted his customs, particularly Christianity. This took place during a period of colonization by the white man, who then assumed control of Maori lands. Like the Hawaiians the Maoris became good churchgoers, wore European clothes and started growing wheat; their traditional social structure was weakened and discord followed. Eventually in 1840, sovereignty was handed over to the British. In the South Island the Maoris were dispossessed; in the North Island they were left with only two-fifths of their land.

This disruptive phase was followed by a period of despair, and during the second half of the nineteenth century the Maori population fell, through disease and warfare, from 200,000 to 40,000. It was a time of withdrawal and rejection: they had lost their *mana* (divine grace) and their confidence in themselves. They had also lost confidence in the white man, his religion and his good intentions.

Then, suddenly, there was a general improvement. The population grew from 40,000 in 1890 to 64,000 in 1926 (in 1951 it was 116,000). Gradually Maoris began to take advantage of opportunities for employment and education. *Maori-tanga*, an attitude resembling *négritude* in Africa, which broadly was a movement to express the values of Maori culture, was encouraged by an intelligent leadership. In due course the Maoris regained their self-confidence through a rediscovery of their heroic past and their traditions, art and folklore. This renaissance manifested itself in the increasing popularity of tribal gatherings, the erection of buildings for community needs and a general feeling of healthy pride.

They even synthesized a new religion. In 1864 they renounced their conversion to English Christianity and made up their own religion based largely on borrowings

Solomon
Islands

top Kapauko warriors of New Guinea
gather in groups to plan battle tactics.
Although the island is now mostly pacified,
a deep-rooted appetite for inter-village
warfare survives in several remote areas.
Wars were traditionally thought to increase
a people's welfare and happiness as well as
improving relations with the dead – by
avenging the ghosts of those slain in earlier
battles. **above and left** The spear-filled
corpse of a Jalé warrior; **left,** a Jalé village
prepares for war. The Jalé, living in isolated
valleys, had no contact with the outside
world before 1961.

above The Bishop of Melanesia speaks to a circle of the converted in the 1890s. Contact with Christian ideals brought a cultural landslide in many parts of New Guinea, causing initiation rites and other age-old customs to be abandoned. On the whole, though, New Guinea has benefited from enlightened administrators and church officials, with the result that new ways have become grafted on to the old without totally destroying the latter. **above right** A New Guinea village in the late nineteenth century. Villages originally consisted of a circle of women's houses built around the men's house in the centre, where all the men ate and slept, only visiting the women for sex. But with the arrival of Christianity the old conventions fell into disuse and the men moved into the women's houses. **right** White men rally to the flag, watched from the other side of the fence by a group of natives. In the nineteenth century the annexation of New Guinea began with the Dutch, who took the western part of the island in 1848; Germany took the north-eastern sector and Britain the south-eastern in 1884. Later Papua, in the south-east (see map) came under Australian control in 1906 and New Guinea, in the north-east, became an Australian mandate in 1921 and a trust territory in 1946. The jointly administered land of Papua-New Guinea is now on the verge of independence. The other half of the island is known as West Irian and passed in 1963 to Indonesia, by whom it is still administered.

from the Old Testament. The Supreme Deity was called Jehovah and the Maoris declared themselves to be one of the lost tribes led into bondage by the Assyrians. Te-Ua, one of their prophets, regarded himself as the new Moses and declared New Zealand the Promised Land and the Maoris its chosen people. Movements like these combined both Christian and native influences and promised the coming of the Messiah, the revival of the Maori dead and the expulsion of the whites. These promises were never fulfilled, but the movements served the purpose of reviving Maori pride and their sense of the past, and gave them hope for the future. They were also accompanied by more practical political action by such groups as the Young Maori Party.

The Maori renaissance came about because there was a revival of the idea of leadership among the Maoris themselves. Eventually a happy amalgam of indigenous and white culture was achieved. The Maoris accepted European technology, education and welfare, but refused to overstrain their community life and organization in case it should break down altogether. Theirs is a success story, the triumph of integration over assimilation, and the picture in New Zealand is certainly happier than the scene of total loss that has occurred in Hawaii.

New Guinea

Modern examples of adaptation to the white man's world through a revival of native leadership are to be found in the New Guinea area. There almost three million Melanesians live on the second largest island in the world and on many smaller islands and island groups. There primitive societies live by the sea and in the mountains, and are sharply divided from their neighbours by language and cultural differences – hunters living beside but separate from large agricultural settlements, sailors beside groups of land-bound peasants. Yet the similarities between them are significant: most have subsistence farms and grow yams, sweet potatoes and sago as their staple crops; and all keep pigs. Native life revolves around farms and ceremonies to stimulate the harvest.

Probably the most significant common trait possessed by the peoples of New Guinea is their acute interest in novelty. Unlike the Australian aborigines and the Brazilian Indians they do not automatically suspect strange goods and strange men. Instead of hanging their heads and hiding behind trees, the boys and men of tribes which have never before seen white men show an unquenchable interest in their clothes, their equipment and their ways: they reveal, also,

left Life on stilts near Port Moresby, capital of the jointly administered eastern region of Papua-New Guinea. **above** Natives selling copra by the basket to a white dealer; one of the chief reasons why life in New Guinea has adapted well to the arrival of the white man is that both civilizations were naturally acquisitive and shared a long tradition of trading with their neighbours. **above right** A scene from the coffee trade; coffee is one of the leading exports of the eastern sector of the island. **right** A waterfront slum in Port Moresby, one of the more depressing by-products of the white man's presence but one that exists on only a comparatively small scale in New Guinea.

great eagerness to acquire these things for themselves. This attitude stems from the fact that, despite New Guinea's inhabitants having come so late into contact with the outside world, and despite their so-called primitivity, they have always been great traders, using many different kinds of money and ceremonial currency to buy the goods, rituals and dances which were traded between settlements. Though isolated from the white man, they were certainly not isolated from each other, and intricate trading networks linked mountain tribes with the coast, and mainlanders with island inhabitants.

This is one important reason for their continuing survival in the twentieth century. Their indigenous exchange economy and their appreciation of private property meant that they did not have to be taught market values (as Robinson taught the unfortunate Tasmanian aborigines on Flinders Island), and so they met the capitalist colonialists on their own ground. Prestige and status were measured by a man's wealth, not by his age, as in aboriginal Australia; wealth was counted in such currencies as shells, ornaments, dogs' teeth, porpoises' teeth and pigs' tusks as well as perishable goods such as the pigs themselves, yams, taro, sago and bananas.

Land of the Big Men

New Guinea was the land of Big Men. That was the name given to the local self-made leaders; they were powerful and wealthy men, shrewd and alert to all economic opportunities. The Big Men were the focus of a capitalist system and their economic expertise was also used on behalf of the community. Their status, like the status of any wealthy capitalist in Europe and America, depended on their shrewdness and material possessions; they displayed their wealth in magnificent feasts. They received help in their transactions from young men who were attracted to their service by their prestige. The Big Men were also the priests and politicians of the village. Big Men in mythology were credited with the ability to make gardens fertile and their earthly representatives were considered to possess *mana* as well as skill and wealth. They used their ritual powers when trading voyages were undertaken and they were also most powerful sorcerers, causing droughts, diseases and famine. They also saw to the initiation of youths.

Big Men were battle leaders in those endemic wars for which New Guinea has acquired a considerable reputation. Before pacification (a 'civilizing' process that has been going on since the turn of the century) a constant state of warfare could be said to have existed between neighbouring communities that were often of the same culture and the same language. The Dani, for example, were divided into some dozen alliances all of which were potential enemies of the others. Warfare, however, was rather a stately, ceremonial affair. Between traditional enemies who were neighbours there was a no-man's-land, marked out at each end by tall wooden look-out towers – a few minutes' run apart – from which frontier guards kept watch. All Dani men were fighters – and professional fighters at that. Most old men had some war wound: a blind eye, a deformed leg, a vivid scar.

There were two kinds of battles: one was a ceremonial encounter, the other a raid. The former, which might only last one day, was preceded by magical ceremonies; then there followed fierce fighting at which as many as twenty clashes took place. At the end of the day the members of each side sat down on their own edge of the no-man's-land and roundly abused their foes. While this kind of battle was highly stylized, rather in the manner of a dance, raids were fearful attempts to take lives, and were usually instigated in order to avenge a death; these had no formality.

Now most of New Guinea is pacified, these wars having been put down by an Australian administration whose government has been involved in the much more horrific war in Vietnam – a war that has seen the slaughter of thousands in one day. Yet Dani wars, which claimed the lives of less than a score of men each year, were part and parcel of that people's way of life. In a large measure people's health, welfare and happiness depended on the pursuit of aggression against their traditional enemies; the wars also heightened the people's sense of obligation to their ghosts and ancestors: until the ghost of a dead man was avenged, both people and crops were believed to suffer.

The ending of the wars affected their rituals: the offering of a cannibal victim in particular ceremonies was no longer possible, because the person to be eaten had to be someone taken in war. How were the natives meant to cope? A pig was substituted for the human victim, but everyone knew that a pig was a pig and a man was a man. . . .

Other changes followed quickly. New Guinea villages consisted of a row or circle of women's houses, and the men's house; the latter was an imposing structure where all the men ate and slept, the women only being visited for sex. But as soon as the ceremonial houses were abandoned as a result of the disturbance to their traditional organization and allowed to fall down, the men moved into the

left An Australian film unit and their Duna guide. The picture is from *New Guinea Patrol*, a documentary film made in 1957. The inquisitive eye of the camera was welcomed in New Guinea where, unlike many primitive communities, in Brazil and Australia for example, curiosity has always been considered a perfectly natural characteristic. **below** The market place at Mount Hagen in the Western Highlands; goods for sale include tomatoes, peanuts, sweet potatoes, pandanus fruit, eschalots and sugar cane.

right A New Guinea family on the move with their now-familiar clutter of western possessions. below Twentieth-century uniforms, arms, drill and tactics for the descendants of Stone Age warrior peoples.

women's houses. Sexual taboos were forgotten. Village ceremonial came to an end because there was no longer a secret place to perform it away from the eyes of the women. Half the population within ten years of contact became Christian. Initiation rites were abandoned. The Australian magistrates stamped out idolatory and forced people to grow new crops. What has been the effect on the New Guinea people? Have they withdrawn into stagnation and apathy like the Australian aborigine and the Brazilian Indian? The answer is that, on the whole, they have not.

What were the reasons for this? In the first place, as we have already mentioned, New Guinea values emphasized the benefits of change. Moreover the natives never had to share their land (and their wretched climate) with settlers avid to farm it. The missionaries too, were comparatively liberal, and tried to retain native customs wherever they were compatible with Christianity. On the whole they made it their policy to allow education rather than conversion to raise the natives from their pagan state. Finally New Guinea, at least in recent years, was blessed by enlightened administrators, whose attitudes were epitomized by one of them, Hubert Murray. In the context of native customs, he declared, 'We may think it a good thing that [the customs] disappear but they have during many generations been the protection of men and women in times of stress and trial and, when these customs and traditions are weakened, the morale of those who have to battle through life without them must surely be weakened.'

Drastic Change in Manus

New Guinea changed, and not only for the worse. Manus, in the Admiralty Islands, a group of islands to the north-east of New Guinea, offers a good example of a people who underwent drastic change within the short space of a generation, but without suffering the total destruction of their cultural pride. The society of Manus was fully studied twice by the American anthropologist Margaret Mead, once in 1928 and again twenty-five years later. In 1928 she found nearly two thousand 'nearly naked savages, living in pile dwellings in the sea, their earlobes weighed down with shells, their hands still ready to use spears, their anger implemented with magical curses, their morality dependent upon the ghosts of the recently dead'. By 1953 they had become neatly-dressed Christians living in uniform American-style houses all arranged in careful rows. 'They were potential members of the modern world with ideas of boundaries in time and space, responsibility

New Guinea tribesmen call in at the store.

to God, enthusiasm for law, and committed to trying to build a democratic community, educate their children, police and landscape their village, caring for the old and sick and erasing age-old hostility between neighbouring tribes.'

The Manus had taken their culture apart and put it together piece by piece. In 1928 they had an elegant and highly patterned culture; they wore grass aprons and the men had their hair in great knots or combed out in haloes. The women often paraded in costumes of shells which dragged heavily on the ground. They had a trading economy and their houses were well-stocked; each man exchanged, worked and saved with the aim of becoming a Big Man. Then everything began to change: along came the European trader, the administrator and the missionary. The Manus began to work on plantations, while their response to the Christian faith was immediate and enthusiastic. Most importantly the 1940s brought the Pacific War: during that time as many as one million American servicemen passed through Manus and provided its people with

an unforgettable spectacle as miles and miles of barracks were built on the spot, from wood sawed in sawmills set up in the bush. They watched the Americans knock down their mountains, blast channels, smooth islands for airstrips and tear up miles of bush with their marvellous machines. They also found that the soldiers treated them like brothers, sharing their meat and ice-cream. The Manus were impressed. They explored everything with great curiosity: the clothes, the American's goods and, particularly, his machines – engines which cut down trees, engines which did everything. The hospital also impressed them. The Manus, mentally alert and adaptable, and predisposed to change – as witness their evident delight at mechanical achievements – were won over by civilization.

Real change in Manus began after the war when a leader, Paliau, who had been a sergeant in the police force during the Japanese occupation of Rabaul in New Britain, returned to the Admiralty Islands and persuaded his people to join in a rebellious movement. He urged on them a campaign of non-co-operation with the Europeans; at

above A Papuan family in the garden of their government-built house. **right** Beneath a portrait of Queen Elizabeth II, a local government meeting takes place in New Britain; the ties and short haircuts of the councillors symbolize their conversion to the democratic processes of the white man.

his instigation the people demanded participation in the affairs of the Roman Catholic Church, and their men refused to work the plantations except at impossibly high wages. Paliau soon had about a third of the thirteen thousand natives of the Manus district under his influence. He gained support from immigrants who needed land, which they could not obtain from landowners, and from younger men who wanted the abolition of bridewealth and who were looking for modern and constructive channels for their energies outside the framework of traditional agriculture.

Paliau was blamed by the Europeans, whose hostility to the native leader was bitter and total, for the activities of a cargo cult known as The Noise. Cargo cults were movements which had swept New Guinea from time to time since the 1890s. Known as 'cults of despair', they are said to have originated in the natives' hopeless envy of the white man's wealth and power. But these natives were not content merely to sit still and wait for the slow processes of education and economic advancement to take their course. They aimed at a rapid acquisition of European goods, and

also of European-style power. The movement encouraged visions and hysteria, among which were prophesies that heralded the arrival of ships and aircraft sent by the spirits containing huge cargoes of non-traditional (i.e. European) wealth. The cults promised an immediate Utopia; they throve on dreams, massed dances, 'miracles' and magical or supernatural behaviour. In some places aerials were erected on tall poles and messages were sent to the ancestors. These ancestors, who were white like Europeans, were expected to return and platforms were set up in villages and loaded with presents in readiness for their arrival. The natives dressed up in European clothes and waited.

These cults had a political element in that they often called for the expulsion of the whites; and the latter always brought repressive measures to bear against them. Yet while the cults rejected Europeans they were certainly not rejecting European civilization. They occurred in areas where the natives were quickly acquiring new appetites for European goods; these could only be obtained by working for Europeans on plantations often situated far from their villages. In the native view the whites received their goods by magical means. They evidently did not manufacture them; they apparently did no work themselves, yet they refused to share their fortune with the natives, forcing them to work hard and long for only a small proportion of the goods with which he was surrounded. Furthermore the natives decided that the goods could hardly have been made by the lazy white man; they must therefore have been created by the spirits of the dead. As part of the consequences of these cults much of traditional New Guinea culture was abandoned. Ceremonial objects were burned, for example, and children no longer had their noses and ears perforated and their hair was cropped short. The hysterical element could be interpreted as a kind of catharsis among the general frustrations arising from changing social conditions and the overthrow of old-established ways. There was no desire just for a return to the past; in Manus the natives wanted to move into the new world. Pagan religion was wiped out, and in the new world the natives followed the white man's style of living.

In Manus the natives' version of the cargo cult, known as The Noise, had many of the usual elements. Village census books and the hats of government-appointed officials were burned; people became seized with twitching and saw visions; traditional property such as shell money, dogs' teeth, mourning costumes, grass skirts, dancing spears and pottery were hurled into the sea, although some were later retrieved. Even the skulls of the dead, so impor-

On these pages are featured some of the thousands of warriors who gather every two years to dance at the Mount Hagen Show. **top** A blue-faced Kandap man. **above** The delicately decorated face of a Wabag warrior. **far right** Dance of the Mud Men, a ceremonial performance that recalls a famous tribal victory when the ancestors of these warriors emerged caked in mud from a river and so frightened their enemy by their ghostly appearance that the latter fled the field. **right** Young Duna tribesmen wearing initiation wigs made from dyed human hair; these men are dressed for a different occasion — to celebrate the opening of a new airstrip at Koroba, in the Southern Highlands.

tant in the traditional Ghost Cult, were thrown out. Cargo ships and aircraft were said to be on their way and docks and landing places were built. Later the inevitable failure of the cargo to materialize produced a violent revulsion, and the government finished the affair by arresting the leaders. This was after Wapi, the prophet, had been murdered by his disappointed brothers.

But Paliau's movement was never associated with the excesses of The Noise. His work was of a more practical nature. He moved inland villages to the coast and pile villages to the land; he established village councils, organized communal food supplies and built up financial reserves. His most remarkable achievement was to persuade the traditionally hostile inland folk to co-operate with the seafarers. He promoted peacefulness, good neighbourliness, hygiene and sanitary improvements, the wearing of clothes and better housing and schools for teaching his ideas. Paliau's success was tremendous, but his anti-European attitudes led to his arrest and his movement was accused of terrorism, the desecration of churches and the burning of administrative records. Nevertheless village councils of the kind he had campaigned for were set up and when he was released he co-operated with the government.

By 1951 the whites had changed their tune and spoke of him as a popular figure who had carried out his duties enthusiastically and intelligently as chairman of a particular village council. The council raised £2,328 in taxes in 1951–2 and spent it on education, health, agriculture and water supplies. A co-operative for the marketing of copra was set up and a traditional store established. In 1953 the United Nations mission found there 'one of the most orderly, progressive and prosperous communities that it had encountered anywhere in the Territory'.

Paliau and leaders like him are the kind of leaders needed to push Stone Age communities into the twentieth century. While the old culture must not be completely rejected, it seems important that changes should be fairly comprehensive and should include the provision of schools, new houses, different clothes, and new cultural patterns to suit such amalgams of native and European ways.

In New Guinea, while there may have been hysterical cargo cults and rebellious movements like those of Paliau, there was not the full-scale cultural depression and apathy found among Australian aborigines and Brazilian Indians. Nor were European customs blindly adopted, but evaluated with careful attention to their suitability and practicality. Modern techniques were adopted quickly if their value was understood. In Papua the men quickly turned to growing coconuts and making copra. Plantation labour was possibly better than the old drudgery, but working one's own plantation was infinitely better; consequently small, privately owned coconut groves grew up around villages. One coastal village bought a cutter to transport its produce to market. Another opened a bank account. In addition to their busy economic life, church-going gave many people fresh heart. In New Guinea the spiritual beliefs of others were not, as often happened elsewhere, excluded or regarded as automatically invalid; as a result Christianity became grafted on to traditional native religion. In many ways Christianity, football and commerce have now successfully replaced the old passions for warfare and head-hunting and for initiations and feasting.

Vive la Différence!

The Manus and Maoris are peoples who refused to be over-awed by the white man. Conscious that society could be changed, they adapted western technology and ideas to match their own needs, but without sacrificing their own culture. They may be Christians, wear short hair and farm with tractors but they have not become a hundred per cent Australian, American or Anglo-New Zealand. They have a pride in their independent ethnic traditions, and provide concrete proof that total assimilation to white men's ways need not be the only desirable aim.

Yet we have allowed a thousand exotic cultures to die without regret. Today we spend time and money bewailing the extermination of such creatures as the rare whooping crane and the sea otter, or the lizards of the Galapagos Islands. Millions of pounds are spent on excavating the remnants of dead cultures; almost nothing is given towards saving living ones. If we do not do something now our children will blame us for allowing the wonderful diversity of mankind to become merged greyly into the neutral, monotonous world of Euro-American civilization. At least until recently our industrial democracy had a single powerful credo to justify its actions: civilization implied progress, while the primitive life conjured up paralysis and backwardness. The slogan of traders and missionaries and

administrators was, generally, that 'Primitives must go'. This, being translated, usually meant: 'People not like us, who do not have our material wants, who do not believe in our Christian God, must go'.

Today people are beginning to realize that the sameness that results from a world-wide melting-pot policy is not desirable. My plea in this book is for differences between peoples to be not only tolerated, but encouraged. Today we can aim to build a society in which different groups can live together side by side.

Throughout the world the prestige of the west is waning, along with our old gods of Progress and Civilization. Many people are inclined to agree with Franz Fanon, a passionate defender of oppressed peoples, that Europe is 'brutal, brilliant, successful and dead'. We have come to reject the myth of the difference between civilized and primitive, and no longer believe that we are God's chosen people. Primitive society is in the news; and many people have decided that technologically inferior groups living in darkest Africa or the blazing savannah of Australia, may enjoy a better

'life style' than ours, and that their values are better adapted to the twentieth century.

We have discovered that simple societies often have cosmologies and thought systems which are just as complex and just as abstract as ours. But we may have discovered it too late. As Australians, Americans and Brazilians begin to make a cult of the art and customs of the indigenous inhabitants of their lands and tourists and anthropologists plague their poor remnants without mercy, the objects of our interest are ceasing to exist. The qualities which we learn to appreciate and admire are those which the advance of civilization destroys. Yet we are looking to primitive man for help in different aspects of our life: today artists draw inspiration from his sculpture and painting; educationalists acquire new knowledge in child-rearing and sexual behaviour, and psychologists and doctors learn new techniques for curing the sick and the insane from those they call witchdoctors and herbalists. On a different level, hippies and Bohemians adopt the dress and even the religions of formerly despised peoples. Back-to-nature has hit the civilized scene. Thousands of nudists move into private parks and beaches (while missionaries export boat-loads of our second-hand clothes to Africa and Polynesia). Public opinion is being influenced by the current revolt against the consumer society, a change symbolized by the new cults for the primitive and natural.

The tables are being turned, and more and more we have a lurking suspicion that the naked primitive, lacking the advantages of our science and our gods, may have known a happier and saner world.

far left Worried faces among New Guinea voters as a candidate for a seat in the House of Assembly puts his case. **above** A meeting of tourist and native in American Samoa. Tourism and the expansionist demands of our Euro-American civilization threaten the future of every simple society on earth. But perhaps there are also grounds for hoping that future generations will prize the values of different and exotic cultures more highly than we do today. Or is it, already, too late?

Index

Acknowledgments

The Editors gratefully acknowledge the courtesy of the following photographers, publishers, institutions, agencies and corporations for the illustrations in this volume. All maps were prepared by Ivan and Robin Dodd and drawn by Geoffrey Watkinson.

Front Cover
The Sunday Times: Don McCullin
Back Cover
The Sunday Times: Don McCullin
Front Flap
Claude Lévi-Strauss
Title Page
David Moore: Transworld Feature Syndicate Inc.
Chapter 1
6–7 The Sunday Times: Don McCullin
8 Radio Times Hulton Picture Library
   Japanese Embassy Library
9 Popperfoto
10–11 Transworld Feature Syndicate Inc.
10 Mike Andrews
12 Museum of the University of Pennsylvania
   Drum
13 Courtesy of the American Museum of Natural History
14 John Bulmer
15 Camera Press: John Seymour
   Drum
16 The Mansell Collection
   John R. Freeman
18 Mitchell Library, Sydney
19 John R. Freeman
   John R. Freeman
20–21 John R. Freeman
      Rex Nan Kivell Collection
      National Library of Australia, Canberra
21 From the Collection of Dr C. Craig
22 Trustees of the British Museum
24 John R. Freeman
25 Radio Times Hulton Picture Library
26–27 Mitchell Library, Sydney
Chapter 2
28 Trustees of the British Museum
30 Trustees of the British Museum
   Trustees of the British Museum
31 Radio Times Hulton Picture Library
   John R. Freeman
33 Rare Book Division: New York Public Library
34 John R. Freeman
   John R. Freeman
35 John R. Freeman
37 Camera Press
38–39 Copyright: The Royal Society & the Royal Geographical Society
40 Camera Press: Douglas Botting
   Copyright: The Royal Society & the Royal Geographical Society
41 Claude Lévi-Strauss
   Chris Menges: Transworld Feature Syndicate Inc.
42–43 The Sunday Times: Don McCullin
44 Adrian Cowell: Transworld Feature Syndicate Inc.
45 Camera Press: Douglas Botting
46 The Sunday Times: Don McCullin
   The Sunday Times: Don McCullin
47 Copyright: The Royal Society & the Royal Geographical Society
   The Sunday Times: Don McCullin
Chapter 3
48–49 Bernice P. Bishop Museum, Honolulu
50 National Portrait Gallery, London
51 The Mansell Collection
52 The Mansell Collection
52–53 The Weaver Smith Collection
53 Hamlyn Group
54 Hamlyn Group
54–55 Museum of the American Indian
55 Camera Press
57 Hamlyn Group
   Burk Uzzle: Magnum
58 Australian News & Information Bureau
   Australian News & Information Bureau
59 Australian News & Information Bureau
   Australian News & Information Bureau
60 Camera Press
61 Australian News & Information Bureau
62 Radio Times Hulton Picture Library

63 Australian News & Information Bureau
   Australian News & Information Bureau
65 Camera Press
   John R. Freeman
66 David Moore: Transworld Feature Syndicate Inc.
   Australian News & Information Bureau
67 Camera Press
68–69 Camera Press
69 Australian News & Information Bureau
Chapter 4
70 Popperfoto
   Camera Press
72 John R. Freeman
   Trustees of the British Museum
73 Honolulu Academy of Arts
74 Bernice P. Bishop Museum, Honolulu
75 Popperfoto
76 Popperfoto
   Popperfoto
77 Bernice P. Bishop Museum, Honolulu
78 Popperfoto
79 Romano Cagnoni
   Robert Goodman: Black Star
80 Honolulu Academy of Arts
81 Popperfoto
   Popperfoto
   Barnaby's Picture Library
82 Barnaby's Picture Library
   Gene Anthony: Black Star
83 Robert Goodman: Black Star
84 Barnaby's Picture Library
   Barnaby's Picture Library
85 Camera Press: Tim Royce
Chapter 5
86–87 Philip Burnham
88–89 Dominique Darbois
90 Philip Burnham
90–91 Philip Stevens
91 Philip Stevens
92 J. Allan Cash
93 Dominique Darbois
94 The Royal Geographical Society
95 Philip Stevens
96 Dominique Darbois
97 Dominique Darbois
   Dominique Darbois
98 Philip Stevens
98–99 John Picton
99 John Picton
101 Colin Turnbull
102 Colin Turnbull
Chapter 6
104 Romano Cagnoni
106–07 A. H. & A. W. Read, Wellington, New Zealand
108–09 Trustees of the British Museum
109 Trustees of the British Museum
110–11 Klaus-Friedrich Koch
111 Camera Press
   Klaus-Friedrich Koch
112 John R. Freeman
112–13 The Royal Commonwealth Society
      The Royal Commonwealth Society
114 John Bulmer
115 Australian News & Information Bureau
   John Bulmer
   The Sunday Times: Don McCullin
117 Australian News & Information Bureau
   Australian News & Information Bureau
118 The Sunday Times: Don McCullin
   The Sunday Times: Don McCullin
119 The Sunday Times: Don McCullin
120 Australian News & Information Bureau
120–21 Australian News & Information Bureau
122 The Sunday Times: Don McCullin
   The Sunday Times: Don McCullin
123 Transworld Feature Syndicate Inc.
124–25 Australian News & Information Service
125 Romano Cagnoni